Praise for S

"A comprehensive an of practical magic. It is truly a treasure trove of information and advice thoughtfully designed to benefit the novice spellcaster."   —Gerina Dunwich, author of *Wicca Craft*, *Exploring Spellcraft*, and *A Witch's Halloween*

Spellcasting
For Beginners

About the Author

Michael Furie (Northern California) has been a practicing Witch for over seventeen years. He began studying witchcraft at age twelve and at the age of seventeen officially took the oaths of the Craft. An American Witch, he practices in the Irish tradition and is a priest of the Cailleach.

To Write to the Author

If you wish to contact the author or would like more information about this book, please write to the author in care of Llewellyn Worldwide, and we will forward your request. Both the author and publisher appreciate hearing from you and learning of your enjoyment of this book and how it has helped you. Llewellyn Worldwide cannot guarantee that every letter written to the author can be answered, but all will be forwarded. Please write to:

Michael Furie
℅ Llewellyn Worldwide
2143 Wooddale Drive
Woodbury, MN 55125-2989

Please enclose a self-addressed stamped envelope for reply, or $1.00 to cover costs. If outside the USA, enclose an international postal reply coupon.

Spellcasting

For Beginners

A Simple Guide to Magical Practice

MICHAEL FURIE

Llewellyn Publications
Woodbury, Minnesota

First Edition
Ninth Printing, 2020

Book format by Bob Gaul
Cover design by Ellen Lawson
Cover photo © Llewellyn art department
Interior art © Llewellyn art department
Editing by Amy Quale

Llewellyn Publications is a registered trademark of Llewellyn Worldwide Ltd.

Library of Congress Cataloging-in-Publication Data
Furie, Michael, 1978–
  Spellcasting for beginners: a simple guide to magical practice/
Michael Furie.
      p. cm.
  Includes bibliographical references and index.
  ISBN 978-0-7387-3309-8
1. Magic. 2. Charms. I. Title.
  BF1621.F87 2012
  133.4′4–dc23
                              2012030555

Llewellyn Worldwide Ltd. does not participate in, endorse, or have any authority or responsibility concerning private business transactions between our authors and the public.
  All mail addressed to the author is forwarded, but the publisher cannot, unless specifically instructed by the author, give out an address or phone number.
  Any Internet references contained in this work are current at publication time, but the publisher cannot guarantee that a specific location will continue to be maintained. Please refer to the publisher's website for links to authors' websites and other sources.

Llewellyn Publications
A Division of Llewellyn Worldwide Ltd.
2143 Wooddale Drive
Woodbury, MN 55125-2989
www.llewellyn.com

Printed in the United States of America

Contents

To my Mother, to Dray, and to the wisdom of witches—past, present, and future. Thank you always for enriching my life. Blessed be.

Introduction

The full moon rises up over the tall, pale birch trees on the side of a cliff, dark ocean waves crashing against jagged rocks far below. Thirteen mystical, otherworldly cloaked figures dance maniacally around a roaring bonfire on the cliff's peak, throwing herbs into a bubbling cauldron and chanting their spell in a long-dead language. The scent of burning oak wood and their magical brew drift into the night air ... sound fanciful? Over the top, you say? It is. Mostly, but this is what so many of us were conditioned to view as the type of scenario in which magic exists: an outrageous, overly complicated, irrational, stereotypical production.

As a child, this was what I believed it took to work magic. I was very focused on fantasy stories about witches and magic. No matter how much my mother (who is magically minded herself) tried to point out reality, I was captivated by the overly dramatic notion of magical practice. Unfortunately, I did not have either the means or the interested friends needed to perform such feats. When I got older and began to study real magic, I read about complex group rituals, which discouraged me. When I attempted to make these rites work in my own way, I became disheartened by my failure to do so. Luckily, my mother was there to give me a little guidance. With her help and a better class of books, I was able to grow and progress both spiritually and magically.

The good news is that true magic doesn't need to be overwhelmingly complex. It took me a while to realize that rituals and spells must be simple and direct in order to be the most effective. In fact, the most important "ingredient" in any work of magic is the training and knowledge of the practitioner. That being said, it is still possible to have enjoyable, theatrical, suitably "witchy" rites as long as the meaning behind the process of the ritual is fully understood. There are basic requirements for every worker of magic to study, learn, understand, and master in order for rituals and spells to be successful. Fortunately, a witch's training can be both an enjoyable and an enlightening experience.

This book is written from the perspective of a witch, and the training and magic found herein is part of the magical heritage of the craft. This knowledge may be used by anyone, as long as slight alterations are made to suit personal faith and one takes the time to thoroughly master the training materials. No one who wants to learn these secrets should be denied the opportunity. In this book, you will learn how to properly meditate for magic; how to prepare for rituals; all the details of what, when, why, and how to work magic; and, of course, spells—lots and lots of spells. In fact, there are over fifty spells and rituals in this book covering candle magic, charms, crystals, witch bottles, poppets, and much more. I hope that you will find this to be a thorough training manual and useful grimoire (spell book). Included are a wide range of magical intentions and tips on creating your own spells. This book has been arranged so that one may first undergo the training and then learn traditionally based spells and recipes in order to work true magic.

Part I

Magical Theory

The use of magic stretches back before history was recorded. Magic was first practiced to ensure bountiful crops, robust health, fertility in both humans and livestock, security, and protection from possibly malevolent unseen beings such as the fairy folk. Over time, as magical practice grew and progressed, guidelines for its successful use developed. As the needs of people changed, the goals of spellcasting evolved as well. Spellcasting now includes such things as love magic, money magic, beauty magic, luck magic, and so on. In this modern age, witches take a more scientific approach to magical study. Witches are taking into account specifics of why magic works: what forces are unleashed, how we focus the power, and how we project it. This way of magical practice has yielded some very interesting discoveries to add to the body of magical knowledge collected over the centuries. Many of these magical methods and practices will be examined in the following chapters.

Training

It has been said before by many that if you ask thirteen witches to define magic, you will get at least thirteen different responses. The same holds true if you ask them for a definition of witchcraft, Paganism, Goddess, etc. Witches are individuals by nature and the lessons acquired from walking this magical path of individualism are truly transformative. Once you undergo the training outlined in this book, you will likely be a very different person than you were before. Your connections to the world around you will be broadened, your senses will be heightened, and your personal power will be greatly expanded. The ability to work magic is a skill that is gained as a by-product of expanding your wisdom and understanding of the natural processes of life. I define *magic* as the science and process of projecting emotionally and intellectually charged energy into the spiritual plane in order to manifest change in the physical world. This practice is a lot simpler than it sounds as long as you are fully versed in the correct methods and given complete understanding of how and why these methods work.

Given the fact that witchcraft is an individualist path, it would appear to be a challenge to teach its ways to others. After all, how do you teach someone to be an individual? The answer is simple: give the student guidelines and tools and let them find their own process. In other words, tell them what to do and why it works, then get out of their way and let them experience how to do it. The basics of magical training include learning the following skills: timing, correspondence, discipline, intent, preparation, magical meditation, projection, grounding, and silence. Let us now examine each of these skills separately.

Timing

To the witch, the universe is seen as a single organism birthed of the great Goddess out of her energy; all beings are connected not only to her but also to each other. We believe that everything in existence consists of energy that is vibratory in nature, both particle and wave. As each creation in the universe (star, planet, human, animal, plant, etc.) interacts with each other, their vibratory patterns can influence each other and create change. A natural example of this can be seen in the nature of gravity. Newton's law of universal gravitation states that every object in the universe attracts every other object with a force which is directly proportional to the product of their masses and inversely proportional to the square of distance between their centers; this means that the larger the object and the closer it is to another object, the greater its gravitational force will be. This law of gravity shows that objects carry their own force and ability to influence the nature and future of other objects.

What on earth does that have to do with magic? Well, magic uses spiritual energy and spiritual energy works according to its own set of scientific laws. Spiritual energy is contained in all things and its intensity and nature vary according to the natural cycles of the physical object or being in which it resides (human, plant, animal, metal, star, planet, etc.). To work magic successfully we must work according to natural law. Magic is in fact a physical science, and this is why certain rules and procedures must be followed to achieve the desired result. We are all gifted with spiritual energy and this energy has its own type of mass, albeit a delicate mass. Our focus and intention act as our own form of mental gravity that we can use to harness the energy and direct it to our goals.

This is where the importance of timing comes in. Spiritual energy ebbs and flows according to natural cycles and using this observation, we have learned to time our rituals and spells to coincide with specific points within these cycles. Put more simply, we practice positive, growth-related magic during the waxing of the energy cycle and negative, introspective, dissolution-related magic during the waning of the energy cycle. The waxing of an energy cycle is from the cycle's point of beginning to its peak of strength; the waning of an energy cycle is from just after the peak of strength down through its decline back to the "zero point" where it began. In an act of magical alignment, witches fuel their spells with the proper flow of energy based on its point in the cycle. This cosmic dance is most clearly seen in the monthly phases of the moon. How does someone know when the waxing or waning times of the energy cycle are occurring? The answer is through the observation of natural phenomena.

The first and largest sign of nature's cycle is the season. Witches are very connected to the earth and our religious rituals are (partially) in celebration of the cycle of birth, life, and death reflected in the turning of the seasons. Witches in the Southern Hemisphere may choose to follow their own natural cycle, or may choose to simply adapt to that of the Northern Hemisphere. In the Northern Hemisphere, the calendar year begins in winter, the time of hibernation, sleep, and seeming death. Winter is dominated by the power of earth—cold, solid, stable earth at rest. It is the key waning time in nature's cycle. As the year moves forward, the season of spring begins. This is the time of the first stirrings of new life. It is the beginning of the waxing time of the year. Spring is dominated by the power of air—warming, windy, sweeping-away-the-gloom air. The season of summer comes next and is the key waxing time in nature's cycle. In summer we have the fullness of life. The power of life is at its greatest strength. Summer is dominated by the power of fire—hot, dry, lively fire. Finally, after the power of life has reached its zenith, the cycle begins to wane and the time of decline begins to emerge with the autumn. Autumn begins the waning half of the year and is dominated by the power of water—flowing, rainy, dewy water. The waxing half of the year is naturally more attuned to magic intended to be constructive: love, prosperity, growth, luck, etc. The waning half of the year is naturally more attuned to magic intended to be introspective, destructive, or dissolving: inner psychic work, bindings, banishments, etc. That being said, I would not advise someone to wait until October (in the northern hemisphere) or April (in the southern hemisphere) to cast a spell to dissolve a chronic ailment (a spell best done during a waning period) if there is immediate need.

The second means of observing and utilizing the universal cycle is through astrological correspondence. In astrology the planets of our solar system (as well as our moon and some asteroids) carry certain qualities and characteristics that correspond to aspects of our everyday lives. Jupiter, for example, is related to growth, expansion, luck, and wealth. These planetary natures are significant as well as their interaction with one another. These interactions are known as "aspects"; charting these aspects can become a lifelong area of study. Astrology is the system of observing the movements and interactions of heavenly bodies and relating their interplay to the cycles of our everyday lives. It is an intense discipline that a magically minded person can use to gain an understanding of universal energy tides and the most propitious times to work various types of magic. This is a worthwhile area of study that will lead to a deeper level of magic and a greater connection to nature's cycles; however, it is a very complex system and requires years of study and practice to fully master.

Fortunately, there are other ways to tap into the correct cycle of nature's power. The third and most often-used method of attuning to nature's energy cycles is to time your work according to the moon. The moon is more than just earth's only natural satellite; it is a source of power and a key component of life. The moon controls the tides; affects the natural cycles of plants, animals, and humans; and in its waxing and waning, it provides energy shifts that we may align with to amplify our magic.

Just as with the seasons, the waxing phase of the moon is the best time to work magic for positive and constructive ends. During the full moon, the constructive power of the moon is at its strongest because it is at the peak of its waxing phase and opposite of the sun. In relation to magic, both positive and constructive spells can be used to indicate "good" or "white" magic such as spells to improve luck or find love. Positive magic is very similar to constructive magic and both are often used interchangeably; a distinction should be noted in that constructive magic is designed to create something as opposed to merely increase a thing or situation already in existence. Fertility spells are a great example of constructive magic. Positive spells are more specifically used to increase or build up something, such as a relationship, a business, etc.

During the waning phase of the moon, it is best to work magic for negative and destructive ends. During the new moon, the destructive power of the moon is at its greatest because it is at the peak of its waning phase and aligned with the sun. Both negative and destructive magic can be used to refer to hexing- or cursing-types of spells, but negative magic can also be used to refer to any magic that creates decline or deals with the past, releasing, or banishing (releasing of negativity such as shame, doubt, stress, weight, fear or phobias, etc.). Destructive is more specifically related to magic designed to end something (such as ending a relationship, destroying illness, quitting smoking, etc.). Negative implies "to remove" whereas destructive implies "to destroy"; this is a subtle yet sometimes very important distinction.

Another useful method of magical timing is working according to the days of the week. Each day of the week has an associated planet, color, energy, etc. that can be utilized to enhance magical practice. Monday is the day of the moon, a day for psychic work and connecting to Goddess energy, the feminine divine forces of the universe. Tuesday is the day of Mars, a day for action, masculine energy, and more aggressive-type magic. Wednesday is the day of Mercury, a day for communication, mental improvement, and learning. Thursday is the day of Jupiter, a day for expansion, luck, and influencing people in authority. Friday is the day of Venus, a day for love, beauty, and partnership magic. Saturday is the day of Saturn, a day for grounding, binding, and dissolution. Sunday is the day of the sun, a day for energy, strength, healing, and connecting to God energy, the masculine divine forces of the universe. (For further magical associations, please refer to Appendix Two on page 231).

Correspondence

Every item used in magic is utilized for its specific pattern of energy. "Correspondence" is used here to mean similarity or equivalence between two or more things. Different energy patterns have influences over different areas of life; because it is scientifically known that energy cannot be created or destroyed but can only change form, it is understood that the greater energy of the universe is expressed in our immediate environment; this is what is meant by the term "as above, so below." The power of the macrocosm is equally expressed in the microcosm of our everyday lives.

Items and objects that bear resemblance to or are related to one another in some way usually carry similar energy patterns. For example, roses and peach blossoms are botanically related to each other and both have energy that has love-enhancing properties. Additionally, various planets, colors, herbs, stones, and metals that share similar qualities and energies have been grouped together accordingly in what are known as *tables of correspondence.* A table of correspondence can be very useful in developing your own spells and recipes as the table shows which ingredients are in harmony with your magical goal. When designing a spell or ritual, it is always best to only use items that share similar energies; otherwise, you will send out a mixed message and the efficiency of your spell will be decreased. Tables of correspondence are included as appendices at the back of this book.

Altar

Another way in which magical correspondence is utilized is in altar arrangement. Altars are used as a focal point for our magic, to hold the tools and ingredients of our spells and give us an energetic center from which to begin our magical process. This helps to focus, program, and release the power of the spell. During outdoor ritual, often a bonfire or a tree would serve a makeshift altar with items being placed at the base of the tree or burned in the fire to release the energy of the spell. Indoors, an altar would be created on a table or a dresser.

Many people see an altar and assume that the items placed upon it are set in a random pattern or arranged to be aesthetically pleasing; this is not so. Altars should be arranged according to the patterns of energy flow and with the tools placed at their most powerful and appropriate places. This creates a circuit of energy and results in more effective spell work. The following tools carry certain patterns of energy and are used to bring influences to our altars and into our lives: cauldron, cup, knife, wand, pentacle or altar stone, and censer. Let's examine each tool and its individual functions separately.

Altar Tools

	Cauldron: The cauldron is a round pot that preferably has three legs and is made of iron. This vessel is seen as a representation of the Goddess and the realm of spiritual energy. It is a sacred grail of transformation and is used to hold objects and candles during spells or (sometimes) to cook holiday meals or brew potions.
	Cup: The cup is seen as another Goddess symbol and as a vessel of the element of water. The cup carries with it all of the qualities of the water element: love, psychic ability, healing, sleep, dreams, the feminine force, and so forth. The cup is used to carry water or wine for toasts, cleansings, and blessings.

Knife: To most modern witches, this is known as an *athame* (ah-thuh-may) and is a large, double-edged, black-handled knife used primarily to direct energy. The knife represents the masculine force and is companion to the cup. To some it is seen as aligned to fire; to others (myself included), it represents the power of air and all the qualities of this element (the mind, thought, influence, communication, etc.).

Wand: The wand is usually a straight, sanded, and blessed stick of wood used to direct energy, in healing rites, and as an invocatory aid. Wands are sometimes made of metal and set with crystals. To some, the wand is seen to represent air; to others (myself included), it represents the power of fire (it is made of wood, after all). The power of fire carries with it the qualities of force, change, sexuality, action, creation, destruction, protection, etc. The wand is a symbol of masculine energy.

Pentacle or Altar Stone: A pentacle is a disk or platter that has been painted or engraved with a pentagram (five-pointed star with the point up) and any other symbols important to its owner. An altar stone is either a large stone used as an altar, a small quartz stone placed on the altar (such as a crystal ball), or a stone platform on which to stand during ceremony. No matter which of these is used, all represent the power of earth and bringing things into the realm of physical reality. Pentacles in particular are used as platters on which to set talismans or other objects to be consecrated or magically charged. Sometimes an offering plate is used in place of a pentacle or stone.

 Censer: A censer is a container in which incense is burned during ritual. On occasion, the cauldron can double as a censer. Burning incense carries the energy of your intent out into the realm of air and is used to lend atmosphere and energy to aid in the manifestation of your goal. Ritually appropriate incense recipes will be given in Chapter 14.

Please note that the tools are not absolutely essential. The most important part of magical work is the intent, determination, and emotion of the spell caster; the tools are just an added focus or boost to the power that comes from within.

Altar Arrangement

The altar itself should be arranged so that when you are standing in front of it, you are facing north. In my work, I use the cauldron to define the center as the spiritual nexus point where all forces come together. Energy is drawn in from the left side of the altar and flows to the right. Tools and items designed to attract energy are placed on the left side of the altar and tools and objects that project energy are placed on the right side. In some cases, this means nothing more than a darker candle on the left, a lighter shade of the same color candle on the right, and perhaps some herbs or a crystal sitting on your altar. Altar design should be a personal creation. Remember that adjustments to suit both taste and necessity can be made in the creation of your own altars at any time.

In the traditional sense, there are ideal circumstances for your altar. A Goddess image of some sort should be placed at the back of the altar in the middle with the censer being placed before her, in between the image and cauldron. A platter, pentacle, stone, or offering plate should be placed below the cauldron, in the middle of the altar. In the upper left hand corner of the altar, a bowl of sea salt should be placed to neutralize any energy that is not in harmony with your goal. A black candle should be placed to the left of the Goddess image; this candle will be an altar candle and will help draw in energy. To the left of the cauldron, another candle should be placed that is in the appropriate color to draw in the specific energy matching your goal. To the left of the platter, a wand is placed with a crystal tip point facing right. Finally, in the lower left hand corner of the altar, there should be a cup filled with blessed saltwater. This helps draw in nurturing energy and will be used to cleanse your working space.

Now that the left side is complete, we move on to the right. In the upper right hand corner of the altar, place the container of incense that is to be burned during your spell. To the right of the Goddess image, place a white candle. This will be your other altar candle and will help project your energy. To the right of the cauldron, place another candle in an appropriate color (a lighter shade preferably) to project the energy of your desired goal. To the right of the platter, lay your knife with the point of the blade placed facing right. Lastly, in the lower right corner of the altar, set your altar stone (if you have one), crystal ball, or small pentacle to bring in the energy of the earth and help ground your rite into reality. Any other additional materials should be arranged on the appropriate side of the altar according to personal taste. This altar design is mostly utilized for full-fledged ritual and isn't necessarily needed for every spell. There are many simple spells in this book that won't require elaborate altars. Just keep in mind the circuit flows from left to right.

Typical altar layout

Finding the Right Altar

Don't stress too much about having a pristine altar space in your home at all times. Any small table, dresser top, or TV tray can be used as an altar. Outdoors, a cleared spot on the ground or an old tree stump could be used. The same holds true for the tools. You do not need to have expensive, elaborate tools to make magic work. Any knife could be used as an athame as long as you feel drawn to it and you charge it as an athame; just don't use it for any other purpose. For a wand, you can use any tree branch. To substitute for a cauldron, you could use a black bowl. For a pentacle, you can paint a pentagram on a plate and charge it (see Charging Ritual on page 75). For a cup, use any cup you wish, though a goblet-style cup with no handle is best. Again, just charge the tools and don't use them for any other purpose beyond the magical. If you use a dresser top for your altar space, you could store your tools in a drawer of the dresser for convenience. Remember: The level of intent and desire are the most important elements in magic; the tools and altars and other trappings mostly serve to focus and enhance your ability rather than being essential ingredients in and of themselves.

Discipline

When I refer to "discipline" in magical practice, don't worry— I'm not talking about intensive martial arts training or learning how to go into deep trance states. Discipline is used here to mean both the training required to ensure proper skills and the calm, controlled state needed to work successful magic. The way to learn proper discipline is to first thoroughly study the training material and then put what you have learned into practice. Practicing the training exercises is key to achieving the proper mental state required for magical work. To ensure regular practice, it is best to set up a regular schedule in which to do the exercises. Any skill is better than no skill at all and each time you practice you will become stronger.

Another way to build discipline is to keep a magical journal or "book of shadows." In this journal, keep a daily record of goals, meditations, insights, dreams, and results of psychic exercises and spells. You could write down any recipes or special skills you acquire as you progress or you can note these in a separate book if you develop a specialty such as tarot or herbalism. The journal is best kept every day to ensure regular practice and it is a good idea to reread it every now and then. You may be surprised how far you've come and how much you have learned along the way.

Witches are taught to be diligent in their journaling. The concept of a book of shadows has evolved over the last few decades. Originally, it was solely a book containing the rituals, spells, and teachings of a coven or tradition held securely by (usually) the high priestess of that coven. This has changed for the most part, and now each witch keeps her or his own book of shadows that is usually part ritual manual and part journal filled with notes and writings as a witch learns, grows, and advances in their craft. In most modern covens, each trainee witch is required to have a blank book (or something similar) to journal and keep notes. Most solitary witches also keep such a book. As with any magical journal, more than one book will probably be needed over the years. Personally, I have two books of shadows—one containing all of the rites and lore from my tradition and another one filled with my personal rituals, spells, and notes.

Intent

Intent is the most important element in magic. Having a clear intent is what activates any spell. The catch here is that it must be a *clear* intent. You need to have a well thought-out and precise result in mind before you attempt to cast a quality spell. You also need to incorporate various safe guards into the spell so that the results will be as intended, without the occurrence of undue mishaps. For example, casting a simple love spell without an idea of the type of person you wish to attract could result in a wide range of people becoming attracted to you. This sort of thing is usually a result of sloppy spell work. To avoid this, it is a good idea to spend some time thinking and writing about your goal. Try to come up with a clear statement of purpose; write a sentence or two about why you wish to do the spell and what result you want to achieve. Do not focus on the process of *how* your goal "should" manifest itself. Witches are taught to get out of the way of the process in order to speed the magical results. Simply focus on your goal and trust that whatever process is necessary will occur to bring about the desired outcome. It is a good idea to state that the outcome of the magic shall be for the good of all. This helps to minimize negative results.

Remember that there is a natural law in which energy sent out eventually returns to the sender. This is the law of return and is inescapable; what goes around does indeed come back to you! Another thing to keep in mind is that when you cast any type of spell on a person, you forge (or rather strengthen, as all things are already connected) a link between yourself and the one on whom the spell has been cast. This link is the means through which the spell travels to affect the spell's target person. This spiritual link can be a pathway for the person to affect you; whether consciously or unconsciously, the other person has spiritual access to you. This can be an unpleasant side effect of using magic to affect people. It is better overall to use magic to alter situations rather than trying to change the human will.

Proper Use of Magical Intent

Magical intent is, as previously noted, one of the most important facets of working magic. For the magic to be ideal in its success, the intent must not only be properly focused and projected but also fit the goal of the spell. For example, if you cast a protection spell designed only for spiritual or psychic protection, you may still be vulnerable to physical attack. If the intent of a spell is not complete or proper in its scope, the effects of the spell will be diminished or diverted. I will give examples and corrective measures for the main goals of most magical practitioners. Let's start with love magic.

Love: Before performing a love spell, you should be able to define as precisely as possible the type of person you wish to attract. You should evaluate whether or not you are ready for a long-term relationship or if your true goal is merely sexual fulfillment. In the case of sexual fulfillment, I would suggest modifying the love spell to only include positive sexual attraction and take out any references to lasting partnerships or lifetime commitments. Be wary of using magic to fall in love if you want to be in love just for the sake of being in love.

Gaining love should not be a means of relieving boredom or to appease a nagging parent. Any magic that involves the lives and free wills of other people should be done with extreme caution. If you only wish to meet new people, to have "a fling," or to have a casual relationship, do not use a spell designed to bring you a true love or ideal mate. If you desire to be in a relationship with another person and you choose to use magic to bring this about, you really need to be sure of your motive and commitment level so that you can avoid a relationship that is more than you are prepared to endure.

Love spells, by their very nature, are potentially dangerous. It is highly inadvisable to cast a love spell on a specific person. This is an outright attempt at overpowering the free will of an innocent human being and would result in negative consequences. In order to cast a spell on another living being, they either have to subconsciously allow it to affect them or you have to channel enough energy to overpower their subconscious shielding (which every being has) and force them into compliance. A spell of that magnitude is harder to cast than you might think when using positive energy, and the more energy you send out the greater the eventual return. If you send out an enormous amount of energy designed to break the free will of another, that energy will return to you. In this type of case, you shouldn't expect the relationship (or anything else) to go according to your wishes for a long time; you will become someone whose free will continually gets overpowered. Relationships created in such a compulsory manner usually don't last long because the target's subconscious mind is aware of what you did, causing resentment and conflict to eventually bubble to the surface and destroy the relationship. If you tamper with the free will of another person, you are, in effect, cursing them. The consequences of casting a curse can be very unpleasant.

The proper intent for a love spell would be to focus on the type of partner you wish to attract into your life with the desire that it be for your mutual good and with free will. This type of love spell, if properly cast, will be free of harsh side effects.

Money: Money is interesting; it is, in fact, artificial. The concept of money is one of agreed-upon value; everyone agrees that a certain coin or piece of paper is worth a given amount and ... *POOF!* It is. Truly understanding that money is more of a perception or concept as opposed to being the most powerful factor in existence is the key in using magic to bring money. Don't get me wrong, having money is important! But not for its inherent value, for it has none. Money is important only because of the security that its agreed-upon value can bring, and that alone.

Now, I'm not saying that if we personally stop believing that money has value in our lives our need for it will stop or that money is a bad concept; rather, I am saying that money is a neutral concept, a symbol that takes on the energy we assign. Prior to the use of money, the barter system was used to trade goods and services. This system was quite cumbersome and would be totally unworkable in today's society. Today, money symbolizes what we crave: safety, health, comfort, and security. This is why there are money spells in magic. We must work within the modern system in order to achieve the life security that only money can provide.

Money magic is about growth, security, and abundance—not money for money's sake. Magic in general works best if there is genuine need (as opposed to selfish want). If you need money for something, cast the spell for that something. If you merely want one hundred thousand dollars for the fun of it, well, you can try for it but trust me, it will be much harder to achieve.

When working with spiritual forces to acquire a mundane, physical thing, it is important to focus on what the exact desired goal is rather than thinking in general terms. Specifically, when using magic to bring money, focus on why you need the money, what it will be used for, instead of just trying to "draw in money energy." We must focus on the truth behind things and not just a thin veneer or a means to an end. Focusing on the money itself is akin to overanalyzing the process of how magic will manifest a goal (which hinders the process). The true worth of money is what it will be used to obtain, and that is what should be focused on. If you need money to purchase a new car, focus on the need for the car. You may also focus on the specific amount of money needed to purchase the car, if desired. Do not however, only focus on the money!

Healing: When working healing magic for one's self or others, it is necessary to visualize the person in a relaxed, healthy state. In your mind's eye, "see" the person healthy and with no illness as opposed to seeing them becoming healed or growing in strength. Surround them with healing energy and state that the injury or illness shall no longer exist. Visualize only the outcome; don't focus at all on the process of healing. Focusing on stages of the healing process lead to projecting confusing signals, causing delays or mixed results. Any healing magic must be done with a true sense of compassion and love infused with it. This maximizes its effectiveness, as magic done without proper feeling is only marginally successful at best.

Protection: As noted earlier, the type of protection magic worked is integral to its success. You should work magic for psychic protection if: you feel that someone is trying to work negative magic against you, a dark spiritual entity has become attached to you in some way, or you fear you're spending time around an energy vampire (a surprisingly frequent occurrence where a group or individual is usurping your energy). If on the other hand, you are worried about physical danger, work magic for physical protection. If you are under immediate physical threat or danger, you should first take all necessary mundane precautions like locking doors, calling police, going to a safe public place, etc. Most people work protective magic as an additional precautionary measure to avoid any such threats. I personally feel that it is a good idea when using protection magic to aim for a combination of both types of protection (both psychic and physical) to make sure you are truly secure.

When working protection magic, you should be filled with a sense of safety and serenity and infuse this serenity into the spell (no fear!). If you are filled with fear, you will only infuse that fear into the spell and it will offer no protection; rather, it will increase the fear. For effective protection, you must project how you want the end result to feel.

Binding: This is in an area known as "gray magic" as it falls somewhere between what has been traditionally called white (or "good") magic and black (or "evil") magic. Binding can be used for positive ends, but does involve the overpowering of the free will, which is the black-magic element of the spell. Overpowering free will is a difficult and discouraged practice; it is dangerous. Unless skillfully done (and even then), there could be serious repercussions to the spell caster. Many modern practitioners never use this type of magic and prefer to not even discuss such things because of the danger to the practitioner. Given the fact that we live in an unpredictable and sometimes harsh world, I feel that it is best to be fully armed and knowledgeable with the use of defensive magic. The key here is *defensive*. Bindings should not be done to control another person for some type of ego boost or a cheap thrill. They should only be done to stop a dangerous person or situation from continuing in a destructive way. Additionally, it is possible (but difficult) to bind oneself to help curb negative tendencies or bad habits.

The proper intent for a binding is to visualize the person bound and unable to escape. Then, give them a specific set of commands to follow according to need. You should feel fully in control without malice or fear. Feel as though you are overwhelming the person into giving in to your demands (think angry nagging as opposed to kidnapping and threatening). Bindings do require lots of energy to be effective and if the person's subconscious mind is strong enough to reject your spell, you will quickly suffer the consequences of rebound. This is why this type of magic should be rarely done and only in times of true need.

In a binding spell, the reason for specific orders is twofold. First, it speeds the success of the spell by giving it clear focus. Second, it helps eliminate rebound upon the spell caster, as the stated conditions do not apply to the one casting the spell. For example, if you need to bind a thief, do a binding spell with the specific command that the person will no longer steal the possessions of others; because you are not a thief (hopefully), there would be no rebound of binding your free will. That being said, there is always an energy return from every spell cast and this is unavoidable. This is one reason it is inadvisable to dwell too often in the realms of gray or black magic. You don't need all that negative energy returning to you and disrupting your life.

Cursing: Ah, the most controversial magical topic of them all. Now, this does qualify as black magic, and as such, should only be done under very severe circumstances. To work a curse, you must first be filled with angry, vengeful energy; second, you must be willing to project that energy onto someone else. This will definitely result in dark energy being returned to you, so you must make sure that you are willing to deal with the consequences and that there aren't any other less-severe options (such as binding) that could accomplish your goal. A curse will cause misfortune and misery in the life of spell's target. Unfortunately, to curse another is to curse oneself, so be prepared to be on the receiving end of misery as well.

If the consequences of curses are so awful, why do people use them? Well, they should only be used in times of greatest need. Dark energy travels quickly on this plane. Much more quickly than positive energy; this is the lure of cursing. It's quick and effective magic. Many people become addicted to the sense of power that the use of such magic brings. This is ignorant and dangerous behavior. The only justifiable reason to cast a curse is if someone has greatly wronged you or a loved one with no remorse and intends to continue doing so (either to yourself or others). In such a case, a curse could be used to force a realization of the person's own actions in that person's mind, creating a kind of tortured empathy or filling their life with such chaos and misery that they no longer have the time or the strength to attempt to harm you or anyone else.

You should be very specific in your goals for a curse so that the possibilities of rebound are minimized, much like in the case of binding. Again, even if the curse doesn't rebound upon you, the dark energy will eventually return and you will face the consequences of your actions. To cast the curse, you must be filled with anger and rage and infuse this feeling into your spell. This can be exhausting, as it requires an enormous amount of energy for the proper results to be achieved. The positive magical path is always a safer and highly encouraged choice.

Preparation

It is vital in the art of magic to be properly prepared before beginning any ritual. This includes correctly timing the ritual; developing a clear intent; obtaining and properly charging all the materials and ingredients for the spell; and bathing yourself in blessed saltwater to cleanse body, mind, and spirit. To create blessed saltwater for a ritual bath, simply obtain a cup or so of sea salt and run a tub of cool water. Next, pour the sea salt into the water and swirl it in. Then, close your eyes and focus on the concept of spiritual cleansing. Focus on the idea that the saltwater will purify you of any darkness, blockages, or negative energies. Now, summon power (as you will be taught in a later lesson) and pray to your deity to cleanse and charge the saltwater for your use. Finally, will your energy to flow into the water, filling it with your intent. You are now ready to take your ritual bath. While bathing, make sure that you completely immerse yourself at least once or use a wash cloth dipped in the water on your face, eyes, and ears to make sure that all of your orifices are cleansed and spiritually sealed. To be spiritually sealed means that your aura (personal spiritual energy field) has been strengthened to protect you from any negative energy attaching itself to you and causing any ill effects such as exhaustion, confusion, nausea, etc. After you have taken the bath, you may begin the meditative part of the spell work process.

Magical Meditation

The art of meditation has been taught and practiced for centuries, but it has also been greatly misrepresented and misunderstood. When I first began my training I was under the impression that meditation was very difficult. Each time I tried to meditate, I hated the experience. Many books and teachers will tell you of the importance of meditation and the need for regular practice, yet few will tell you *how* to properly do it. The few who do tell you how to meditate are usually utilizing meditation for goals other than magic, such as relaxation or introspection. For this reason, the benefit of their instruction is limited when it comes to enhancing magical practice. Magical meditation, the type I will focus on, is a slightly specialized form of meditation designed to create the proper mental state in which to visualize and project magical energy. I feel that the need for regular practice of meditative techniques has been overemphasized. This statement will undoubtedly provoke dissenting opinions, but it has been true for me personally. Don't misinterpret my message; regular practice of any new skill is essential to its mastery and keeping a regular schedule will ensure that the practice becomes second nature. However, we must live in the real world here. I have actually read and been advised that in order to be successful at the meditative process, I need to meditate twice every day for thirty minutes each time. I don't know about you, but I barely have time to sleep, let alone meditate for an hour a day!

It was advice like this that caused me to forego meditation completely in my early years. As a result, my magical practice was greatly stunted and my results were spotty at best. It wasn't until I learned the truth about meditation and began to incorporate it appropriately into my life that my training was able to advance and my magic began to grow. For starters, forget all the advice about how often or how long you "should" meditate each day. This is a skill and any skill must be learned and built as a gradual process. Ideally, you should set aside five minutes a day at first and build up to at least fifteen minutes or more, but just go at your own pace. If your schedule is busy (and whose isn't) just meditate whenever you can.

I've also been told that I have to meditate at the same time each day for effective results. I view statements like this as potential stumbling blocks to success. Believing this kind of advice has, in the past, caused me to give up for weeks or sometimes months because I couldn't find the same time each day to meditate. In order to be effective, meditation simply has to put you into a quiet, reflective mode. That's it. All the trappings and spurious advice about it only serves to distract you from its actual practice. Just meditate whenever you can for however long you can. It is true that the conventional wisdom about regular practice is technically valid and would build the skill faster. However, it is more important to build the skill in a way that actually works with your unique life and circumstances than to vainly attempt to conform to an impossible ideal of how the skill "should" be built. Any meditation is better than none at all. We all need to grow at our own pace. Simply do what you can and in time your magic will grow and reward you for your efforts.

Now that I've told how *not* to meditate, the question then becomes, how should you meditate? Just remember that meditation is sort of like returning to your childhood. When we were children, we all used our imaginations much more often than we do now. Meditation, magical meditation in particular, is a means of harnessing the power of the imagination in a consciously controlled manner. The whole process is much more enjoyable when it feels like you are a kid again playing "let's pretend" rather than an anxious, studious, frustrated adult trying to master the art of meditation.

Magical meditation is designed to put you in the magical frame of mind needed to cast spells. It is relatively simple and involves four steps: focus, contemplation, feeling, and visualization. Combining these steps in the meditative process will be the key to all future spell work. Let's examine each step individually.

Focus

Focus is the ability to concentrate on a single task without distraction. For many people, myself included, this can be a very difficult state to achieve. A good way to enhance your ability to focus is to zone out on a mindless, repetitive task. A wonderful method for doing so is to start by holding a string of large beads and counting off each one. While counting beads, close your eyes and imagine an image or sound; it could be each color of the spectrum one by one, the tick of a metronome, or an old-fashioned clock.

It is a good idea to do these exercises with your eyes closed and while in as peaceful a state of mind as possible. If any of these exercises are continued for three full minutes, you will then be in a meditative state of relaxed brain activity referred to as alpha brain wave level. This meditative state is necessary for successful magic. When the mind relaxes, it reaches the deeper level of consciousness needed to connect to realms beyond the physical world. That being said, these exercises can be difficult to perform if your mind has a tendency to wander. When the mind begins to wander, just pull your attention back to the repetitive task and move forward. Don't get upset or be put off by the difficulty. Remember, even if your mind wanders the exercise is not a failure. Each time you try an exercise, you are building these skills stronger and stronger.

They say that it takes twenty-one to thirty days of repeated practice to develop a habit, so I would advise you to make sure not to give up hope before you have tried this exercise for at least that length of time. I assure you, it will get easier and it is truly worth the effort. Focus must be achieved before beginning any meditation, spell, or ritual. After you have gained the ability to appropriately focus, the next step in the meditative process is to begin contemplation.

Contemplation

Contemplation is simply reflecting on, considering, or thinking about something. It is similar to visualization and is indeed the first step toward visualizing something. Truly, not much needs to be said about contemplation, as most of us are rather skilled at it. People contemplate things, other people, scenarios, and events all the time. The only techniques required are focus and a clear idea of the qualities of the subject of contemplation.

We use contemplation in magic before a spell to fully consider all the factors involved in the magic we are about to perform. What situation has occurred that led us to the point of wanting to use magic to intervene, and how do we wish the situation to change as a result of our efforts? Try to focus on as many sensory cues as possible—every sight, feeling, sound, and smell. Thoroughly reflect and imagine as much detail as you can about the subject of your contemplation. Once this is achieved, you can move on to infusing this with your desire.

Feeling

Feeling is a beautiful enhancer to almost any meditation and the most important key to magical meditation. If you focus on feeling a particular emotion during the process, it will help you concentrate, making the meditation easier and more rewarding. In magic, it is of utmost importance that you focus on how you want to feel when the end result is achieved before and while casting a spell. Most people are rational creatures and it is only natural to try and reason everything out. Magic, however, works by different means. Magic is change, and change occurs by the easiest method available. Without focusing on how you want to feel, you run the risk of your spell working in a way that makes you very unhappy but is still technically what you wanted.

Keeping in mind how you want to feel when your goal is reached creates that feeling as part of the criteria of your spell, allowing your spell to manifest in as pleasant a way possible. Emotionless magic is dangerous and (fortunately) frequently unsuccessful. Once you have decided how you want to feel, the next step is to build your visualization of the goal.

Visualization

Visualization, much like meditation, is a term that is often misunderstood. Many people are intimidated by the idea of using visualization and feel it is too difficult to learn or use. Thankfully, the reality is that this talent is delightfully simple to learn. In truth, everyone already knows how to visualize. "Visualization" really just means imagination. All of us are able to close our eyes and imagine a beautiful tall tree with its bright green leaves gently swaying in the warm spring breeze. A strong imagination is much more than the escapism we were led to believe it is; it is a key to creativity, power, and magic.

In meditation, visualization helps us focus and gives our minds something to do such as seeing numbers, colors, images, or scenarios. In magic, visualization is used to conjure up a mental image of the results you wish to create with a spell. Remember, it is only the result that should be visualized, not the means of getting to the result. Get out of the way of the process.

Affirmation

An affirmation is a positive thought or statement affirming that a desired goal has been or is being reached. When I was first starting out as a witch, I scoffed at the thought of positive affirmation. I thought that it was nothing more than an act of self-delusion and pointless over-optimism. It turned out that I was wrong. Affirmation is used in exercises training the subconscious mind and to charge your magic with clear intent.

The subconscious mind is tricky. It tries to block any attempt to consciously control it, but utilizing the power of the subconscious is necessary for successful magic and spiritual enlightenment. There are many methods of training designed to rein in and control the subconscious mind. Each of these methods has three things in common: they all contain the elements of shape, color, and affirmation. These three things (when combined in the proper way) speak to your subconscious and pave the way for communication and eventual cooperation between the two halves of the mind.

In practical magical application, affirmations are used as statements of purpose or spoken chants. These chants, when used with feeling and visualization, combine the rational side of the mind with the intuitive, magical side, and this joining together is what gives you the ability to work magic. As long as you use focus to prepare the mind, contemplate the situation, immerse yourself in how you wish to feel, visualize the result you are working to achieve, and apply a strong statement of affirmation to give clear intent, the process will take care of itself and your magic should be blessedly successful.

Beginning Meditations

The following meditations should serve to bring all of the previous steps together to provide firsthand understanding and development of these vital skills. When starting to work with these meditations, it is a good idea to record yourself reading these out loud and play it back to guide you in the meditation, as having to read the words is distracting and will pull you out of the meditative state.

Star Meditation

On a piece of paper, draw a large pentagram. Now, find a comfortable place to sit where you will not be disturbed and study your drawing. Think about what a pentagram symbolizes: protection, power, the elements, the senses, the human body, and the Goddess herself. Try to feel within yourself what a pentagram means to you personally. How do you feel when you see one? Do you see it as a frightening symbol? A magical seal or a religious symbol? Truly search your feelings for the answer.

It is now time to close your eyes. With your mind's eye, imagine a white pentagram. It helps to let your closed eyes roll upward as if to see through your "third eye" which is located in the center of your forehead. See this pentagram as clearly as you can. Try to make it completely defined. Hold this image in your mind for as long as you can. This will take time and practice to perfect, but I promise you it can be done. The key here is to let yourself go and drift into your own childlike imagination. Try to remember when you were a kid and used to play "let's pretend." Once you clearly see the pentagram say to yourself, "This pentagram shines down on me and fills me with magical power."

After you have successfully created and retained the image of a pentagram over a series of meditations, expand the exercise by mentally changing the pentagram's size and color. You can make it move and rotate, or make it three-dimensional. Imagine it's made out of wood, metal, plastic, or clay. To end the meditation, pass your hand over your closed eyes and mentally dissolve the pentagram, leaving only empty blackness. Then, gently open your eyes.

Rainbow Meditation

This meditation is more advanced and easily takes you into a proper meditative state. First, it is a good idea to have a picture or drawing of a proper rainbow (color one with crayons!) with the outermost band being red, then moving inward through orange, yellow, green, blue, indigo, and finally, violet. Study this picture until you feel that you can easily visualize a proper rainbow.

Make yourself comfortable and close your eyes. Breathe in and out gently and evenly and see yourself outdoors, floating on a cloud. The cloud floats up toward a beautiful rainbow. The cloud takes you directly above this rainbow to the peak of the rainbow's arch. At this point, the cloud begins to slowly descend into the rainbow and you find yourself surrounded by color. You begin to feel the slow descent and your field of vision is colored red. All you see is red as you pass through this part of the rainbow. Slowly, you sink deeper into the rainbow and now your vision changes and all you see is orange. The color glows and feels like being out in warm sunshine. As you drift further down through the rainbow, you move into yellow. Everything is yellow as fresh and bright as daffodils. Moving deeper into the rainbow, you now find yourself surrounded by crisp, spring green. As you continue your descent, you move into beautiful sky blue, then dark, cool indigo. Your journey is almost complete as you finally sink into violet. You are now in the violet sphere of spirituality. Once you are in violet, say to yourself, "I have traveled through the spectrum and have now reached a spiritual level of power and comfort. "Count down from seven to one and settle into relaxation for as long as you wish. To end this meditation, imagine yourself being drawn up quickly back through the colors and out of the rainbow.

Counting Meditation

Counting is a repetitive act that can be somewhat hypnotic if done for a long enough period of time. This meditation is a good method for reaching a calm, relaxed mental state. Before beginning, you must decide how long you want the meditation to proceed and how many numbers you want to count. You will be counting down, so pick a high number from which to begin (at least fifty). To begin this meditation, close your eyes and focus on seeing only blackness. Next, see a white image of your beginning number form in your imagination. Assuming that it is fifty, visualize it clearly and then begin counting down. As you slowly count down from fifty, see the previous number fade away and the next number take its place. It is a good idea to "hear" or "feel" a ticking sensation in your imagination with each number (like the noise from an old clock) as you count down, to deepen the experience. When you have reached zero, you will be in a relaxed, meditative frame of mind. Say to yourself, "I have reached the quiet center of my being. I am protected and connected to my inner power." Drift in this state for as long as you wish before slowly opening your eyes to end the meditation.

Three Cauldron Meditation

Sit or lie down. Breathe deeply through your nose and exhale through your mouth three times. Allow your breathing to return to normal and relax. Now, imagine a small cauldron within your forehead, the location of your third eye. The contents of the cauldron glow with a yellow-gold light; the cauldron is filled with the energy of thought. Imagine a glittering beam of this yellow-gold light coming down from the cosmos and filling the cauldron within your mind with even more light. This light energizes your mind and enhances your mental faculties.

Next, imagine a small cauldron in the area of your chest. The contents of the cauldron glow with a blue-green light; this second cauldron is filled with the energy of emotion. Imagine that a glittering beam of blue-green light shines down from above and fills the cauldron within your chest with even more light. This energy fills you with emotion and gives you an enhanced ability to feel and connect with others.

Then, imagine a small cauldron in the genital area. Within this third cauldron glows a red light; this is the energy of willpower, action, and creation. Imagine that a beam of glittering red light shines down and fills this cauldron with even more light. This energy fills you with power, charisma, and an enhanced ability to merge your thoughts and emotions and create tangible change in the physical world.

Finally, see the three glowing cauldrons; see their light grow, expand, and finally combine until the light covers your whole body. As the light merges together, see it blend into purple light tinged with gold. Absorb this energy into your body, through the pores. When you wish to end this meditation, it is a good idea to release any excess energy by breathing out and imagining that the excess energy sinks into the earth beneath you (through the floor and then into the earth, if indoors) to be recycled. Finally, count up from one to ten in order to refocus back to the material world.

Third Eye Meditation

Sit or lie down. Breathe deeply through your nose and exhale through your mouth three times. Allow your breathing to return to normal and relax. Now, close your eyes and let them roll up slightly in your head as if to stare at your third eye (pineal gland) located in the center of your forehead. Don't force your eyes to do this, just *allow* them to do it. Next, visualize this third eye. See it glowing with an indigo-colored light. This is the color of psychic vision. Then, see a beam of white light stream down and enter your third eye. As this light enters, see the light change color to indigo. This additional light will cause your third eye to glow brighter and begin to pulsate slowly. As it pulsates, you may feel it tingle with power. Either way, as it pulsates, see it radiate this indigo energy and see this energy spread throughout your body until you are completely filled with indigo light. Bask in this light for as long as you wish.

When you want to end the meditation, send the indigo light out of your body, into the ground and slowly open your eyes.

Projection

Projection is the ability to externalize your intent, emotion, and energy and send it out to manifest your goal. It is the "casting" part of spellcasting. In order to properly project, you must work on the previous exercises first (timing, correspondence, discipline, intent, preparation, and magical meditation), and take time to develop the ability to summon and focus your energy. An effective means of summoning energy is to draw energy into your body from the earth. To do this, go outside and stand barefoot (preferably) on the ground or stand before your altar and close your eyes. Breathe in a steady rhythm and visualize beautiful white light being drawn up from the earth, through your feet, legs, and into your whole body. You have now summoned energy. To focus this energy, you simply concentrate on your chosen goal and infuse it with the proper emotion.

The final step is the actual projection. To project the energy is a simple process. After you are filled with the properly focused energy, raise your arms and send the energy out into the sky (or your chosen goal, talisman, candle, etc.) with your mind; visualize it streaming out from your third eye, palms, and fingertips. For me, it helps to take a deep breath, and as I exhale, "breathe it out" and chant the spell.

Grounding

Grounding is a term that refers to the process of willing any residual energy back into the earth and refocusing yourself back into a mundane, rather than magical, frame of mind. To do this, it is helpful to sit or lie on the ground and imagine that your body sends out spiritual roots that stretch deep into the earth. These roots release any blockages or excess energy into the earth. After you feel refreshed, visualize these roots retracting into your body and stand up. The grounding is complete. Another helpful method of grounding is to simply eat a light meal and relax. Sleep also has a grounding effect, so don't worry too much if you forget to ground yourself. After a good night's sleep you will be well grounded.

Silence

Silence is an underappreciated facet of working powerful magic. Silence is very important to the process and is one of the four pillars of magic, also known as the witches' pyramid or four skills of the magus. The four pillars are: to know, to dare, to will, and to keep silent. Most people view the keeping silent part as necessary only in terms of safety and discretion, but silence is necessary to preserve the energy flow of your spell. Magic works by the projection of charged energy; this energy exists as waves that can be altered by your thought patterns and the thought patterns of others. That being the case, it is vital that spells should be told to no one (at least until they are successful). This avoids any disruption by another person's thoughts regarding your spell. Whether someone else's thoughts would be positive or negative is virtually irrelevant. Any type of interference is damaging to your original intent and could alter the success of your spell. Any intent can be disrupted by telling others even a wish on a birthday candle, which is where the advice "don't tell anyone or it won't come true" originated.

Each of the steps and exercises in this chapter may seem daunting and at times difficult to master, but with some practice the exercises become easier and the skills become second nature. Take each step one at a time and move forward at a pace that feels natural to you. When all these steps are combined, you have gained the ability to shift into an "altered state of consciousness"— a topic often referred to in regard to magic and witchcraft. As the following chapter will show, utilizing the whole process in actual spellcasting can be both simple and enjoyable.

two

Putting It All Together

In this chapter, we will explore exactly how to combine all of the training and put it into practical and successful use. First of all, in order to use magic there would need to be a goal. Once we've determined our goal, the next step is to figure out what type of spell we need to use. Is it a positive and growth-related spell such as, "I need more money"? Or is it a negative or dissipating spell such as, "I need to decrease my debt"? Or is it a goal that requires as much energy as possible, such as extreme healing or protection? After we figure out the type of magic needed, we have to figure out when to cast the spell according to proper magical timing. After the timing is determined, we must gather together all the tools and materials needed for the spell. Finally, on the day of the spell, we need to take a cleansing bath, begin our meditation process, and then cast a circle. Once the circle is cast, we may then work the spell we have chosen, open the circle, ground our energies, and lastly, tell no one of our magic (at least until it has been successful).

Let's examine the importance of using a circle in magical work, how to cast one, and how to open one.

The Circle

The circle is a spiritually cleansed and properly prepared area that is used for magical or religious rituals by most modern witches. The magic circle is constructed by first setting up a circular boundary on the floor using such things as cords, flowers, salt, or cornmeal and then projecting energy from your body into this area. The intention is to create a sphere of energy that extends both above and below ground, completely encapsulating the desired working area and those within. Creating a magic circle is a relatively simple process and should be performed prior to any magical ritual. The circle helps to contain and focus magical energy during spell work and blocks out any outside interference.

The method for constructing a circle is a very basic, reliable, modern means of creating sacred space. In my particular tradition, we have a specific means of preparing a ritual area that involves different tools and somewhat different methods. I am choosing to give you the basic method, as it is quite effective and should be easily compatible with most spiritual paths. You will need to gather together all your ritual items and any other participants within the ritual area, as you will be casting the circle around them. Once the circle is cast, everyone must remain within its boundaries. If someone walks through the circle, it will break and the energy will dissipate. The circle would then have to be recast from the beginning.

Circle Casting

Items needed:

- Cup
- Pentacle
- Wand
- Knife
- Bowl of salt
- Saltwater
- Incense (appropriate to your magical goal; see Recipes page 205)
- Red candle (to symbolize the flame of spirit; your inner power)
- Matches
- Stones, ribbons, flowers, shells, or a long cord (to mark a circular boundary)

Procedure

The circular boundary should be large enough that all the participants can comfortably stand within without breaking the sphere of energy. A nine-foot diameter is traditional but not mandatory. After the boundary has been laid, mark the points of the cardinal directions (north, east, south, and west) in some special way. You may use candles if you wish (green, brown, or black for north; yellow or white for east;

red for south; silver or blue for west), flat stones, or some other means to mark the directions.

Generally speaking, it is believed that each of the four directions is connected to one of the classical four elements of earth, air, fire, water, though there are exceptions to this belief. Many (if not most) practitioners of magic see earth connected to the north, air to the east, fire to the south, and water to the west. Specific candle colors are chosen to correspond with these elements. The reason to identify the directions and mark them according to their elemental associations is that we are going to acknowledge and "call" the elemental essences into our circle to lend their energies for both protection and as an aid to our magic.

The next step is to arrange the altar in the center facing north. Place the red candle in the southwest area of the altar. First, light the altar candles, then the red candle, then and any point (direction) candles if used. After everything is arranged and all are ready, it is time to actually cast the circle. This is done by holding the knife in your dominant hand (the one you write with) and while standing within the circle at the north point, going into a relaxed meditative state. When you are relaxed, summon energy and visualize that the energy streams forth, through your body and out of the knife blade as beautiful, electric bluish-white light. When you feel the energy begin to flow, slowly walk in a clockwise direction within the circle holding the knife out to project energy along the circular boundary. You should begin and end in the north. In your mind's eye, see the energy stretch and grow into a sphere that encapsulates the entire circular area within a perfect orb of spiritual power. Walk the boundary while projecting energy three times; as you make the first pass say, "I cast this circle to protect from harm." As you make the second pass say, "I cast this circle to focus our power." As you make the final pass say, "I cast this circle to be sacred space." Each line is an affirmation of your intent and only needs to be stated once, though could be repeated if desired.

When you have finished creating the energy circle, return to the altar and fill the cup with saltwater. Bless the saltwater to neutralize negative energy by holding the cup in your hands and sending your energy and intention into the water. When the saltwater is blessed to your satisfaction, return to the north and begin to sprinkle some of the water around the circle. Again, move around the circle in a clockwise motion, beginning and ending in the north. After sprinkling the water, light the incense and carry the censer clockwise around the circle; then carry the red candle clockwise around the circle as well.

It is now time to call upon the elemental energies to bless your circle. To do this, first stand facing north and call to the energies and essence of the earth element, "Power of earth, I ask you to attend this circle." Try to feel and visualize the earth energy at the north point of the circle. Next, face east and call, "Power of air, I ask you to attend this circle." Again, visualize the power of air draw in at the eastern point of the circle. Then, face south and call, "Power of fire, I ask you to attend this circle." Visualize the power of fire manifesting in the southern point of the circle. Finally, turn to the west and say, "Power of water, I ask you to attend this circle." Visualize the essence of water coming into the western point of the circle. As a visualization, it is good to see a colored mist form above the chosen directional marker (candle, stone, etc.)

after calling that element. You are likely to see green, brown, or black for earth; yellow or white for air; red for fire; and silver or blue for water. Now, complete the circle casting by saying, "The circle is cast. So mote it be!"

Opening the Circle

After casting the circle, your spell can be performed (ideas and instructions for spellcasting later in this book). After the spell is complete, the circle must be undone. To properly open the circle and release its energy, the following rite should be performed.

Standing in the north, hold the knife up and say, "Thank you, powers of the north. I release you." Now, visualize the earth energy dissolving into vapor. Repeat in the east for air, south for fire, and west for water. Return to the north and hold the knife out into the circle and visualize the energy of the circle being absorbed into the knife. Walk slowly around the circle, counterclockwise and say, "I open this circle. May it be open but ever unbroken!"

Cutting a Doorway in the Circle

Sometimes we forget things. Sometimes we forget to silence the phone. Sometimes we get a knock on the door. When these things happen during circle, rather than just walking through the circle and breaking it (thus having to start all over), you can simply cut a doorway in the circle so that you can exit without any problem. To cut a doorway, you just have to go to the edge of the circle's boundary holding your athame. Bend down to the floor, piercing the circle at the point it reaches the ground. Next, visualize some of the energy of the circle being absorbed into the athame and cut an archway in the circle, moving counterclockwise and making sure that it is tall enough to walk through. You have now created a void in the circle that you can step through without breaking it. The rest of the circle's energy will remain intact. When you return; step into the circle and hold the athame at the base of the circle and moving in a clockwise arch, send the energy *back* into the circle, filling in the void.

Once a circle has been cast, you are ready to cast any spell you choose. The circle can be an important component of spell work because the magic circle acts as a container of spiritual energy; helping to focus it and preventing some of it from dissipating before the spell has been cast. Remember, though, that it is not always necessary to create a magic circle to cast a spell. Successful spells can still be cast without an elaborate circle. In fact, you can create a simplified magic circle just by going into a meditative state and visualizing yourself (and your altar area) surrounded by a bluish-white bubble of energy. There are several spells (such as most of the verbal magic section) meant to be cast when needed, on the spur of the moment when there would be no time for a full-scale circle rite.

One last note on the circle: If your altar is against a wall, you can visualize the circle boundary either going into the wall or even extending through the wall to the outside (whether it be a full circle or the simplified magic circle). The important thing when using a circle is that you and your working space are contained within it. Of course, if it needs to go through a wall, just mark the boundary of the rest of the circle, finishing by having the markers run up to the wall, then cast the circle as usual.

Symbolism

Using symbols in magic is another way of utilizing the principle of correspondence. Symbols are a means of connecting to and channeling power from the force that the symbol represents. Symbols contain no inherent energy. They are merely representations of spiritual forces, templates to which we must add power and meaning in order for them to be useful. A symbol speaks to our artistic, right-brained side, the side that works magic. This part of our brain prefers to work with shape and color. This is why we use candles, symbols, and rituals to power magic. These tools speak to our magical side and help us access and channel the necessary power.

Magical symbols have been utilized for centuries. In choosing symbols, it is preferable to use symbols that have stood the test of time and have been found useful and efficient. It is necessary when choosing a symbol to make sure that the symbol has an easily identifiable resemblance to what it is supposed to represent. For example, it would be foolish and most likely ineffective to use a giant lightning bolt symbol when attempting to channel lunar energy as this would have no obvious connection to the moon. A crescent would be the appropriate and obvious choice because the moon more often appears crescent shaped to us.

The study of ancient and modern magical symbols is complex and involved. To begin, I will share a list of common symbols, many of which will be used later in spells in this book. Further research is always encouraged.

Symbols

♀	*Ankh:* The *ankh* is an ancient Egyptian symbol of life, the joy of living, and spiritual power.
○	*Circle:* The circle is used as a symbol of balance, oneness, safety, and enlightenment.
☽	*Crescent:* The crescent is used to symbolize lunar energy and those things over which the moon has influence, such as dreams, psychic ability, water, night, and Goddess energy. The waxing crescent has the points or "horns" pointed to the left. The waning crescent has the horns pointed to the right.
☽○☾	*The triple-moon symbol:* The triple-moon symbol is a symbol of the Goddess showing her changing face (as the Moon Goddess) and her influence over all aspects of life: the waxing, full, and waning phases; maiden, mother, and crone.
+	*Cross:* The equal-armed cross symbolizes the meeting place of magical forces, a nexus point through which energy is drawn. This symbol also stands for control of natural forces, the four cardinal directions (north, south, east, and west), and the four classical elements (earth, air, fire, and water).

	Eye: The eye stands for secret knowledge and clairvoyance; the ability to see psychically.
	Eye of Horus: Horus is an Egyptian god, the son of Isis. His eye was torn out in a battle with his brother Set and torn into six pieces. The god Thoth restored his eye and this symbol is said to stand for healing, protection, wisdom, prosperity, restoration, and resurrection. The eye of Horus is also known as the *Ujat* or *Wadjet,* meaning "Whole One."
	Infinity Symbol: The infinity symbol, resembling a figure eight turned sideways, is a symbol of infinity, eternity, spiritual power, timelessness, interconnectedness and divine perfection.
	Knotwork: The knotwork symbol is a sacred emblem of continual spiritual evolution and enlightenment.
	Pentagram: The pentagram is used to symbolize many things, primarily the four elements surmounted by spirit, the five senses with the sixth psychic sense in the center, magical power, humanity, and the Goddess.

⛧	*Pentagram (inverted):* The inverted pentagram symbolizes the material (the four elements) overpowering and controlling the spirit. This symbol can be used to denote that which is considered evil and can be used in spells designed to bind dark forces through the power of the elements.
☉	*Sun:* The Sun symbol helps success, strength, and protection.
☿	*Mercury:* This symbol aids in communication and studying.
♀	*Venus:* This symbols helps love, beauty, and harmony magic and draws in feminine energy.
☽	*Moon:* The moon symbol helps in psychic work and in drawing forth goddess energy.
⊕	*Earth:* This aids stability, grounding, and can be an "X-marks-the-spot" symbol; it can be drawn or carved as a point through which energy is channeled.
♂	*Mars:* A symbol which helps bring strength, force, protection, and masculine energy.
♃	*Jupiter:* A symbol for abundance, luck, and to influence people in authority.
♄	*Saturn:* A symbol for binding and grounding to reality. Can be a harsh energy.

♅	*Uranus:* A symbol for flashes of genius, surprises, electricity, and modern technology.
♆	*Neptune:* A symbol for dream work, psychic ability, and intuition.
♇	*Pluto:* A symbol of breaking limits. Holds very powerful and sometimes excessive energy. Pluto frequently has very few boundaries and should be used with caution; results obtained can be stronger than desired.
✴	*Seven-pointed "Faery Star":* The Faery Star is a symbol of faery power, the elements combined with the self, and the concept of "as above, so below." It represents luck, the days of the week, and the seven planets of the ancients (Mercury, Venus, Mars, Jupiter, Saturn, Sun, and Moon). These were the only "planets" other than Earth known at the time, so the bulk of magical planetary lore is attached to them.

Spiral: Spirals are the symbol of life, growth, and eternity. The very core of our being is expressed through spirals. The DNA molecule is an intertwined double spiral. The magnetic field of the earth itself is said to be in the form of a spiral. Various places of power such as standing stones and stone circles have magnetic fields in the form of spirals that reverse their polarity after a time. The so-called "cone of power," the magical energy raised by a group in ritual, takes the form of a spiral as well.

Two spirals: These are sometimes drawn together, one spiraling one way, the other the opposite, to form *spiral oculi* (double spirals resembling eyes). As a symbol of the eyes, these are protective, increase clairvoyance, and promote good health and wisdom. As a symbol of life forces, one spiral represents winding into the still center of all things while the other spirals outward from the center back to the everyday world. These are excellent symbols of and for meditation. Used individually, the clockwise spiral represents the positive polarity of the life force, similar to the pentagram, while the counter-clockwise spiral represents the negative polarity of the life force, similar to the inverted pentagram.

	Triangle: A triangle is a threefold symbol of manifestation. Pointed up, it symbolizes ascent, fire, electric manifestation (sending energy out to create change), and growth. Pointed down, it symbolizes water, descent, decline, and magnetic manifestation (drawing things to you). Pointed up with a horizontal line through the middle, it symbolizes the element of air; pointed down with a horizontal line through the middle, it symbolizes the element of earth. These symbols can help draw in the elemental energies if they are drawn or painted (using elemental colors) on flat stones or disks and placed at the appropriate directions in a magic circle.
	Triquetra: The three points of the *triquetra* represent the three realms of land, sea, and sky in Irish myth and legend, as well as birth, life, and death; mother, father, and child; mental, physical, and spiritual; and thinking, willing, and feeling. All the sacred "threes" are illustrated by this sign. It is frequently used as a symbol of the Goddess, each point seen as one of the three aspects of maiden, mother, and crone.

Triskele: The *triskele* is related to the triquetra. This is a symbol of evolution and spirituality, the continual spiraling back and forth of all in existence. "Triquetra" is the Latin word for triskele. The triskele is a more basic form; most are drawn using three spirals or bent arms joined together in the middle, rather than the more complex interlaced patterns of many triquetras. Most of the symbolism regarding the triquetra applies to the triskele.

Zodiac Symbols: These are the symbols of the twelve signs of the zodiac. The dates given for each sign are approximate, as the true astrological dates can vary slightly from year to year.

- Aries (March 21–April 19) ♈
- Taurus (April 20–May 20) ♉
- Gemini (May 21–June 20) ♊
- Cancer (June 21–July 22) ♋
- Leo (July 23–August 22) ♌
- Virgo (August 23–September 21) ♍
- Libra (September 22–October 21) ♎
- Scorpio (October 22–November 21) ♏
- Sagittarius (November 22–December 21) ♐
- Capricorn (December 22–January 20) ♑

• Aquarius (January 21–February 19) ♒

• Pisces (February 20–March 20) ♓

Color Symbolism

Color is used to lend its vibration to spells and rituals. Each color has a specific wavelength and rate of vibration. Using the rainbow as an example, red has the largest wavelength and slowest vibration, which is why it is the outermost band in the rainbow. As you move through the rainbow, each succeeding color (orange, yellow, green, blue, indigo, and violet) has a shorter wavelength and faster vibration. Color has been shown to affect mood and even brainwave levels. People have used different colors and colored light as an aid to healing and relaxation.

Aside from any aesthetic or health-related uses, color has been used in various magical ways for centuries. Charm bags are made from fabric in specific colors, spells are written on paper in colored inks, even gemstones can be chosen according to their color as one means of determining their magical abilities. One of the most popular uses for color in magic is in the use of colored candles in spells and rituals. Certain colors connect with energies and intentions better than others. For example, indigo (midnight blue) is a very good color for connecting to psychic energy because its higher vibration promotes deeper levels of consciousness. Orange, on the other hand, would not promote a psychic state of mind; its larger wavelength is suited for communication and boosting energy levels rather than a relaxed psychic state.

When using different shades of a given color, the darker shades draw in power and the lighter shades project power.

They should be placed on the altar accordingly: the left side (darker colors) and the right side (lighter colors). There are some intentions that have more than one color associated with them; for example, most colors have protective qualities (my favorites are red, white, and black). Below is a quick list of color correspondences to use in magic. See Appendix Two for further information.

Red: fire, strength, passion, courage, protection

Orange: communication, energy, change in accordance with will

Yellow: intellect, divination, learning, persuasion, air (note: clear bright yellow can substitute for gold)

Green: growth, fertility, abundance, love (color of Venus), plants, earth

Blue: water, healing, happiness, peace

Indigo: psychic ability

Violet: spirituality, meditation, higher power

Brown: earth, animals

Black: drawing in energy, dissolving illness or negativity, protection, multipurpose

White: sending out energy, purification, protection, air

Gray: neutrality, stalemate (clear light gray can substitute for silver)

Silver: Goddess energy, dreams, moon magic, intuition

Gold: God energy, strength, sun magic, success, prosperity

Copper: love (again, tied to Venus), beauty

Pink: love, friendship, emotional healing

If you are using colored candles for magic, please note that plain white or natural beeswax candles can be used in place of the colored ones if the colors are unavailable. The colors are an enhancement, and though much preferred, are not mandatory. If possible, you could place the candles in colored holders to still draw in that energy.

Sample Spell

The following example contains practical applications of each of the steps in the previous chapters and should provide you with a complete overview of the (general) magical process. In this example, assume that you want to cast a spell to find your lost cat. Because animals are independent beings with a mind, a will, and a destiny all their own, and because we don't precisely know where the cat is or what happened, it is best to use a spell designed to draw and encourage the cat to come home rather than a manipulative one used to compel the cat back to you against the cat's will. Keeping this in mind, let's use a modified version of the spell "To Call an Animal Familiar" ("familiar" referring to an animal helper of a witch) on page 95.

This spell was originally designed to draw a new animal familiar to you but we will modify it so that it can be used to bring back an animal with which you already have an existing relationship. Since we become very close to our pets, slightly modifying this spell to help bring a dear friend back into our lives should be no problem. Let's name it "To Call Our Cat Home."

Before performing this rite, it is best to clearly remember whatever physical, mental, and personality qualities your lost cat possesses. Make a list of these attributes on a piece of paper and copy it down in your magical journal. Doing so will fine-tune your intent and ensure that your message is sent to the right cat. This spell is best performed on the full moon because this is a time of enhanced psychic ability and you are trying to psychically communicate with your cat.

Items needed:

- Beeswax or dark-brown candle (for the left)
- Beeswax or light-brown candle (for the right)
- List of personality traits along with your cat's name
- Picture or drawing of your lost cat (if you have one)
- Cauldron or heat-proof bowl (to be used as a censer)
- Burning mixture of rose petals, clover (for magic, love, and strength), and catnip
- Quick-lighting incense charcoal
- Familiar oil (for recipe, see page 206)

After you have gathered the ingredients and arranged your altar, you must take a cleansing bath. Then, remember a time when you were with the cat, how much the cat means to you, and all the happiness you shared. This is not a time for sadness or the feeling of loss at their absence; that would defeat the purpose. You must remember the loving familial relationship you had with the cat. Try to feel "warm and fuzzy." The final step of preparation is to use one of the beginning meditations, such as the rainbow meditation, to bring you into a relaxed meditative state. It is now time to begin the spell.

Procedure

It is necessary to first summon energy; then light your altar candles. The next step is to dress each brown candle with the oil (rub the oil from the middle of the candle up to the wick, then from the middle down to the base) as you pour energy and the loving desire to be reunited with the cat into the candles. Brown candles are used for this spell because this color is associated with earth, grounding, and animal magic. It is a color that a cat would naturally respond better to than say magenta or orange. Now, sit before the altar and light the charcoal in the cauldron. Sprinkle some of the burning mixture into the cauldron as well. As the scented smoke swirls, rises, and drifts through the air, study your list of personality traits and visualize your lost cat; feel a deep emotional bond to them. Whisper your cat's name to yourself. See yourself reunited with the cat as though it has already taken place!

When your energy, connection, and visualization are strong, light the brown candles (first the left dark-brown candle, then right light-brown candle) and chant the following spell:

Loving kinship forged in time,
Ally, helper, guardian, friend,
(Cat's name), if you desire to renew our bond,
Follow the beacon that to you, I send.
Only for good and with harm to none,
So I say, this spell is done!

Stare into the dark-brown candles flame as you focus on a "pulling" sense, creating a sort of energy current, a pathway for your cat to reach you. As you do this, look once more on the list of personality traits. Then, light this list in the dark-brown candle's flame and drop it into the cauldron. Say aloud, "It is done." Leave the candles burning for at least one hour (if it is safe to do so).

It is now necessary to ground your energy as you have been taught. Then, after the candle is extinguished and has cooled, gather all the leftover bits from your spell and bury them in the earth. Then, of course, clean and put away your ritual tools.

Don't forget to keep silent about your magical work so as to avoid diminishing your spell's power. You should also go out and look for the cat. All magic must be followed up with mundane actions in order to create the harmony needed for your goal to manifest. If I cast a spell for a new job but then stay in my house for a month, never talking to people or even looking at the classifieds, I cheat myself of the opportunity for my magic to work.

I hope this spell has explained all the steps necessary to work magic and has shown that spells can easily be tailored to your personal needs as long as you are careful in your modifications. Magic is an art, a science, and a way of life. It will take time, practice, and trial and error in order to build these skills. Once these skills are acquired, the ability to work magic is a wonderful and life-changing gift. It is also something that carries a great deal of responsibility. Having the ability to affect situations, animals, and people can become a dangerous pursuit if selfishness or carelessness creeps in. Magic should truly be worked for the good of all.

Even negative magic should still contain blessing elements if at all possible. Likewise, blessings should carry a "for the good of all" caveat so that you don't accidentally bless someone harmful. Yes, even blessings can be dangerous. If you bless someone and they commit some sort of crime, the blessing could act to impede their capture, or worse. To add "for the good of all" or "harming none" or "for only the highest good" into the blessing eliminates any negative unforeseen consequences.

It is a good idea to do this when working magic for others. It is sometimes difficult to judge the true motivations of others. It should be understood that personal gain can be achieved without loss or denial to another and that personal gain is only taboo when one gains from another's suffering. Intentionally causing denial or loss to another is a negative act and should be avoided at all cost. If you work magic for everyone's good as a matter of practice, you automatically eliminate any accidental cruelty on your part. Remember: What goes around really does come back around! It may even return with greater intensity, so it is always in your best interest to strive to work only positive magic, thus ensuring that only positive energy returns to you.

Don't cast any spell simply for practice. If genuine need is not present, it would be much harder to generate the proper focus, emotional connection, and enough power to work the spell. Thoughts, feelings, and willpower must all combine to create the magical spark necessary to work true magic!

Part II

Magical Practice

In Part I, you were introduced to the basics of magical work and have been given the tools and instructions to put those lessons into practical use. Part II is dedicated to the actual working of magic; it is in essence a spell book. All of the primary forms of magical work are included in these chapters: candle magic, charms, witch bottles, poppets, cords, magical rituals, and miscellaneous magic. The most important quality that each of these forms of magic share is that they all are a means of utilizing magical power and programming it with your intent.

Magical Power

Magical power is spiritual energy. It is the power behind all things, the energy from which everything is created. This energy has the ability to absorb thoughts and feelings; this is how magic works. When creating a charm or poppet for example, you are essentially creating a packet of programmed energy that is focused to carry out a desired effect. Spiritual power can reach any distance or goal as long as there is a psychic link; the energy then makes contact through the link to the target.

In quantum mechanics, an effect has been discovered called "entanglement" in which particles that share similar properties can affect one another without having any direct contact. In fact, they can be moved to opposite sides of the world and still influence one another. Some scientists, such as Albert Einstein, were troubled by this and called this phenomena "spooky action." They sought to disprove it, but were unsuccessful. Rather than calling it spooky, a witch would call it magical, a manifestation of spiritual power. In essence, this is the scientific truth behind the ancient concept of using personal items from the target of a spell (such as hair or fingernail clippings) in magical workings. The personal items are the "particles" that still have influence over whom they were once in contact; when combined with other spell ingredients and programmed with magical intent, they send their power directly to the target of the spell regardless of the distance between the target and the spell caster. The magical energy makes direct, instant contact.

In order to make sure that all the energy of your spell is properly tuned, it is necessary to "charge" each of the ingredients of the spell with the correct quality of energy and intent. To magically charge an item means to fill it with magical power and intent so that its own energies are enhanced and match the goal of your spell. In order to charge an item, herb, tool, incense, etc., the following rite is performed.

Charging Ritual

The charging will need to be done according to an appropriate moon phase for the type of charge desired (see moon phase information under Timing on pages 10 and 14).

Items needed:
- Tool or object to be charged
- Incense appropriate to your intention (see Recipes on page 205)

Procedure

Begin by gathering all the tools and items necessary, arranging the altar as usual and taking a cleansing bath. Next, go into a meditation and reflect on your goal for the ritual, i.e., the type of charge you want the item to hold. The next step is to cast a circle and begin the rite.

When the circle has been cast, settle yourself before the altar and hold the item to be charged in your hands (if the item is too large, place it on the altar and hold your hands above it). Close your eyes and see the item in your mind while at the same time, sweeping your dominant hand over the item in your other hand (or on the altar). Say, "I neutralize energy not in harmony with me and fill you with [state intention] power! For the good of all and by land, sky, and sea, as I will, so shall it be!"

Repeat this chant three times and then pass the item over the incense smoke. The charge has been made. The rite can now be concluded and the circle opened. After the circle is opened, wrap the charged items in natural black cloth or fabric in appropriate colors (see Appendix Two) until you use it in a spell. This keeps the item clean, safe, and fully charged until needed.

Dabbling

If you ask any experienced witch or other magical practitioner about the safety of "dabbling" (sampling from various magical systems or only practicing part time), you will frequently receive an eye roll, a shake of the head, and a long lecture about the hazards of being a dreaded "dabbler." The criticism of practicing magic part time or taking bits and pieces of different philosophies and magical systems and attempting to integrate them into a single practice (which can indeed be dangerous) is somewhat justified. Learning to use magic is a lifelong study, practice, art, and craft. One really cannot approach it as a part-time endeavor. A great many people think that if they just "read the right book" and "cast the right spell" the whole world will simply bend to their will and their life will be perfect. On one hand, I wish that were true; on the other hand, if it was true, we wouldn't need to learn or grow as people in this life and most of life's deeper meaning would be lost.

Any system of magic—whether it be ceremonial, eastern, witchcraft, or any of the myriad forms of magical practice—should be learned, understood, and practiced individually at least until one has gained both sufficient experience and the desire to move on to a new system. Each system of magical practice, though perhaps similar on the surface, can contain a vast amount of ritual, lore, and wisdom that is exclusive to that path. If an inexperienced person goes about happily "blending" bits of practice from various parts of the world, blissfully unaware that they might not fit together well, it is a potentially dangerous act. Why? First of all, if the person is a part of American culture, for example, and they choose to mix Santeria ceremony with Buddhist philosophy, their own understanding of each of those systems will be limited, not to mention that Santeria and Buddhism may not blend well together. Conflicting practices, when thrown together, will not work according to plan; this failure of action can create doubt and future roadblocks in the mind of the practitioner. There are many different cultures and spiritual practices with widely varying beliefs, ethical boundaries, and spiritual focuses. For example, in some religions, releasing attachment to material things is a goal; in others, some material objects are prized as sacred. More importantly, the views on deities, life, destiny, and magic can greatly differ. The disharmony created by trying to blend too many belief systems together can diminish the magical effect you are trying to create.

If you focus your energies on creating magical systems instead of practicing tried-and-true methods of magic that have existed for generations, your magical skills will be rudimentary at best. One must gain a certain level of practical experience before knowing what works best on an individual level. You cannot go about randomly discarding ancient wisdom in the belief that somehow you have greater knowledge. Some practices will work better for others than for you (and vice versa). That doesn't invalidate a practice's overall use, just the usefulness for your personal magical efforts.

Secondly, there is another and much greater danger in being a dabbler. This danger is less about magical acts and more about the spiritual side of being a magical person. Many religions, particularly those of a Pagan slant and including Pagan witchcraft, call on various deities during rites of worship and rites of magic; this is known as "invocation." Some people feel drawn to different deities from separate pantheons. The danger in this is that you have to be absolutely certain the deities you call upon are in harmony, not only with you but with one another. If you call on Apollo from the Greek traditions because you want help with a spell for growth and harmony during winter and you also call on Cailleach from the Irish tradition because winter is her domain and you seek her protection and help, you are asking for trouble. In the first place, gods should never be treated as mere ingredients to a spell. To belittle them in such a way is insulting and deplorable behavior. Apollo is a sun god, bright and energetic; Cailleach is a goddess of the dark half of the year and winter's decline. Their energies are totally incompatible, and chances are they are not going to get along very well. To call powerful beings who don't get along with one another can have disastrous consequences for the poor magician. If you wish to invoke chosen deities into your life and into your magic, be very careful about calling on more than one at a time; always make sure that if you do call more than one, they will be happy to see each other.

three

Candle Spells

The use of candles in magic can be a very powerful means of casting a spell. The lighting of a candle can be a very evocative act, and candles play integral parts in magical practice. Candles, lanterns, torches, and bonfires have been utilized in magic and religious ritual for untold centuries. These have all been used ceremoniously as a means of harnessing the force of fire to enhance our ability to manifest our intent.

The element of fire represents transformation and the "flame of spirit"; using fire in the working of magic aids the ability of spiritual power to transform our lives in the physical world. When we charge a candle with both energy and intent, the charge is stored within the candle until the wick is lit; as the wax melts, the charge is released and poured forth from the flame to begin manifesting our desire. The flame of a charged candle transmits the energy of our intent continuously until the flame is extinguished. A candle can therefore be left burning to continue our spell even after we have ceased to transmit our personal energy.

In order to focus your intent before you charge a candle, you may do one of two things: (1) write out your desire on a piece of paper which could then be placed beneath the candle, or (2) write your desire on the candle itself. If you choose to write your desire on the candle itself, starting at the base, carve the words into the wax in a clockwise, upward spiral. After focusing your intent, charge the candle by simply holding it in both hands while summoning power and focusing on your desire; mentally pour this energy into the candle, willing that it stay in the candle until the flame is lit. The charged candle is now ready to be used in the appropriate ritual for your desire.

Candles are anointed or "dressed" with magical oils to enhance their vibration and speed the magic. To dress a candle, first prepare and charge the candle. Then rub oil on the candle starting from the middle and rubbing up to the tip, then again from the middle rub oil down to the base. The candle is now ready for the spell.

The following spells make use of candles and the basic altar setup. A variety of intentions have been included in these pages, but remember that you can modify these spells to suit your own personal needs.

Healing

For this spell, you will need an accurate diagnosis of illness. You will need to remember that you must only visualize the patient (whether you or someone else) in a strong, healthy state from the very beginning.

Items needed:
- Beeswax or blue candle (for the left)
- Beeswax or white candle (for the right)
- Beeswax or colored candle in the patient's astrological color
- Healing oil (see page 208)
- Healing incense (see page 207)
- Cauldron or heat-proof bowl (to be used as a censer)

- Personal item or photo of patient from a healthy state
- Diagnosis written on a piece of paper
- Black ink (or black pen)
- Pin

Procedure

Begin by taking a cleansing bath and then arrange the altar. Once you are settled before the altar, carve the patient's astrological symbol into the candle; while holding their astrological candle, go into a meditation. When relaxed, visualize the patient in a healthy, strong state of being. See them laughing and having fun. Fill yourself with the joy of seeing the person in good health. When this feeling and visualization are at their peak, pour energy into the astrological candle and charge it with a healthy state of being.

Next, place it on the altar and pick up the blue and white candles. Grasp each candle firmly in the proper hand and charge these candles with the energy of healing. Then, with the pin, scratch your desire onto each candle and the symbol of a circle. Anoint them with healing oil and set them back on the altar. Light the incense and gaze at the photo or personal items of the patient while blotting out the diagnosis on the piece of paper with ink or pen. The diagnosis no longer exists. Drop the paper in the cauldron for it to be consumed by the healing power of the incense.

While visualizing the patient in perfect health, light their astrological candle, then the blue candle, then white candle. While lighting the candles, chant:

With no harm, for good of all,
Away from you, the illness falls.
Healthy mind, healthy heart,
Healthy body, magic impart,
Illness purged, spirit cleansed,
All your suffering at an end.

Again, visualize strongly the patient in a healthy, strong state of being and feel as if the healing has already occurred. Keep this visualization for as long as you can, then open the circle. Leave the candles burning (if it's safe to do so) for at least an hour, preferably until they burn out on their own. Bury the remnants of this spell on a Sunday, a day for healing and success.

Purification of Self

To purify oneself is to remove any accumulated negative energy or "psychic grunge" that has built up on your aura and is causing you distress. This is a relatively simple procedure and does not require the usual altar setup; only a single candle, some oil, and a bath.

Items needed:

- Beeswax or white candle
- Purification oil (see page 215)
- Pin
- Lukewarm bath with blessed sea salt

Procedure

Fill the bathtub as usual for a cleansing bath. Once it's full, step into the bath and go into a meditation while holding the candle. When you are relaxed, visualize a strong white light filling you from the top of your head, down your body, to your toes. As this light fills you, any negativity is broken, dissolved, and eliminated by the power of the light. See the light then forming an "egg" of light around you to ensure continued cleansing. When your visualization is strong, charge the candle with the ability to purify you as it burns to dissolve any residual negativity in the general area. Now, come out of the mediation. With the pin, carve a triskele on the candle, light it, and relax in the bath for as long as desired. When the bath ends, drain the water completely while you remain in the tub. Visualize that all negativity is literally going down the drain, leaving you pure, strong, and healthy. Extinguish the candle and anoint the soles of your feet, bend of the knees, abdomen, wrists, back of the neck, and forehead with purification oil. It is done.

To Bring Forth Visions

This candle spell enhances your ability to scry, or gaze into shiny surfaces to receive psychic visions, and can be used with any scrying medium such as black mirrors, pools of ink, water-filled cauldron, crystal balls, etc. The time of the full moon is the best time for psychic work, but divination is used as need dictates.

Items needed:

- Beeswax or purple candle (for the left)
- Beeswax or white candle (for the right)
- Psychic oil (see page 214)
- Psychic incense (see page 214)
- Cauldron or heat-proof bowl
  (to be used as a censer)
- Quick-lighting charcoal
- Chosen scrying medium
- Pin

Procedure

Begin by taking a cleansing bath and meditating on what it is you wish to see or understand through visions. Arrange the altar and light the incense. Anoint the third-eye area of your forehead with psychic oil and grasp both candles, one in each hand (purple in left, white in right). Go into a meditation in which you visualize a beam of white light streaming down to enter your third eye and fill you with the power of clear vision. See that this light streams down into your hands and enters the candles, charging them with the ability to aid your psychic vision. Open your eyes, and with the pin, scratch your desire for visions on each candle as well as the symbol of an eye. Then anoint the candles with psychic oil and place them on each side of the scrying medium, far enough behind and away so that they will not cast a reflection into it. Now, take up or place hands on the scrying medium and breathe your energy and the white light into it, filling it with the power to spark your psychic vision and reveal that which you seek. Finally, gaze into the medium and try to see it as having infinite depth. After a time, images will begin to show themselves and may either be symbolic or actual scenes of the past, present, or future. Be sure to keep notes on what is seen.

To Bring Love

This spell is designed to attract someone to you who possesses desirable characteristics. These characteristic must be very specifically drawn out and expressed during the casting of the spell. Before beginning this spell, you must have a clear concept of the type of person you seek and write down the essential qualities you wish them to have on fresh, unlined paper. You must write down their gender and a preferred age range. Ideally, this spell could be performed on Beltane eve (around the thirtieth of April) while Venus is in a positive aspect, but any night when the moon is waxing or full will do. If you wish to invoke the power of Venus into this spell, you may add a green candle placed behind the cauldron and dressed with love oil when you dress the other candles.

Items needed:

- Beeswax or red candle for the opposite sex, beeswax or purple for the same sex (for the left)
- Beeswax or pink candle for the opposite sex, beeswax or lavender for the same sex (for the right)
- Green candle (optional, if you wish to invoke the power of Venus)
- List of desired qualities

- Love oil (see pages 208-209)
- Cauldron or heat-proof bowl
  (to be used as a censer)
- Love incense (see page 208)
- Quick-lighting charcoal
- Pin

Procedure

Gather the ingredients, take a cleansing bath, arrange the altar, and cast the circle. Once the circle has been cast, sit before the altar holding the piece of paper and go into a meditation. When you are in a meditative state, visualize your ideal mate. Imagine them as clearly as you can. See them already in your life and infuse that image with a gratified feeling of love. Feel the security, joy, and happiness of reaching this goal as strongly as you can. Next, while still in your meditation, summon energy and program this energy by continuing to focus all your thoughts and emotions on your ideal mate. Now, open your eyes, set the paper on the altar, and grasp the two candles, one in each hand (red or purple in left, pink or lavender in right). Pour the magical energy into the candles; grasp them tightly and will that they be charged with this power. Next, with the pin, scratch your desire into the candles. Anoint the candles with love oil. Place them back on the altar and light your incense while continuing to focus on the joyful feeling of love in your life. Look once more at your list of desired qualities and then safely place it beneath the red or purple candle.

When your energy, emotion, and visualization are strong, light the candles (first left, then right) and chant the following spell:

Flames of love burn bright for me,
Enchant someone I shall desire.
Let our hearts merge strong and free,
We now join our spirit fire.
According to free will and for the good of all
A strong, true love, I hereby call.

Again, visualize strongly and feel the love that you are working toward as though you already have it. Keep this visualization for as long as you can before opening the circle, leaving the candles burning (if it's safe to do so) for at least an hour or preferably until they burn out on their own. Fold the list of qualities into as small a square as possible and keep it with you until the spell has worked; once the spell has worked, bury the remnants of this spell in the ground on a Friday, the day of Venus, Goddess and planet of love.

To Bring Needed Money

To cast this spell first, determine what your actual need is and the amount of money needed to achieve it. Next, write down the need on a square of fresh, unlined paper. Ideally, this spell could be performed in the spring and while Jupiter is in a positive astrological aspect, but this spell is best performed during the waxing or full moon.

Items needed:

- Beeswax or green candle
  (for the left, to draw in growth)
- Beeswax or gold candle (for the right,
  to release the energy of abundance)
- Royal blue candle (optional; placed in the
  cauldron to bring in Jupiter's influence)
- Money oil (see page 211)
- Money incense (see page 210)
- Paper with magical need
- Pin

Procedure

Gather the ingredients, take a magical cleansing bath, arrange the altar, and then cast the circle. Once the circle has been cast, sit before the altar. Hold the piece of paper and go into a meditation. When you are in a relaxed, meditative state, visualize your magical need. Imagine it as clearly as you can. See it as already manifested and infuse the vision with a gratified feeling of achievement. Feel the security, relief, and happiness of reaching this goal as strongly as you can. Next, while still in your meditation, summon and program this energy by continuing to focus all your thoughts and emotion on your goal.

Open your eyes, set the paper on the altar, and grasp the two candles (one in each hand—green in left, gold in right). Pour the magical energy into the candles; grasp them tightly and will that they be charged with this power. Using the pin, scratch your desire into each candle. Anoint the candles with money oil. Set them back on the altar with the piece of paper (safely) placed under the green candle.

If you have chosen to use a royal blue Jupiter candle as a third candle, now is the time to charge it. Scratch the symbol of Jupiter on the royal blue candle and anoint it while asking for the power of Jupiter to aid and magnify your spell (Jupiter's power is that of growth, luck, influence, and expansion). Now, with all in readiness, light the incense, the green candle, the Jupiter candle (if used), and the gold candle while chanting:

> *Only for good, shall it be;*
> *Power of growth, shine on me;*
> *Golden magic, now released;*
> *To bring the gift that [I/we] need!*

Again, visualize strongly, and feel that which you are working toward as though you already have it; focus not on the money, but on the need for the money. Keep this visualization for as long as you can before opening the circle. Leave the candles burning (if it's safe to do so) for at least an hour, or preferably until they burn out on their own. Bury the remnants of this spell in the ground on a Thursday, the day of Jupiter.

To Bring Peace

This spell is designed to calm angry tempers and return a home to a peaceful environment. This spell may need to be repeated often (each moon cycle, perhaps) in order to keep the peace.

Items needed:

- Beeswax or light-blue candle (for the left)
- Beeswax or white candle (for the right)
- Peace oil (see page 211)
- Peace incense (see page 211)
- Personal item from each family member
  (or photo showing every resident of the home)

Procedure

First, take a cleansing bath. Arrange the altar and then go into your meditation. When relaxed, visualize a storm subsiding over the ocean and see the ocean become calm and still. Then, gradually transfer that image into one of your home. See your home filled with calm, still, peaceful energy and soft, blue light. Feel an inner sense of tranquility and ease. When your visualization and emotion are strong, charge the candles with peaceful energy. Scratch your desire for peace into the wax and dress the candles with peace oil. Light the incense and as you gaze upon the picture or items from the family, visualizing them all coexisting peacefully. When your visualization is at its peak, light the candles (left then right) and chant:

> *The currents calm and spirits rejoice,*
> *Harmony fills body, mind, and voice.*
> *Terrible storm, cast away*
> *Our peaceful life, here to stay.*
> *By free will, for good of all, and harming none,*
> *So I say the battle is done.*

Again, visualize strongly and feel the peaceful home life you wish to bring as though it has already occurred. Keep this visualization for as long as you can before opening the circle. Leave the candles burning (if it's safe to do so) for at least an hour or preferably until they burn out on their own. Bury the remnants of the spell on a Friday to promote love or a Wednesday to promote communication.

To Enhance Spirituality

This spell will create a new sense of spirituality and oneness with all things. It will open your mind to greater awareness.

Items needed:

- Beeswax or violet candle (for the left)
- Beeswax or pale blue candle (for the right)
- Spirituality oil (see page 215)
- Spirituality incense (see page 215)
- Statue, picture, or symbol of a beloved god or goddess
- Pin

Procedure

First, take a cleansing bath and then arrange the altar. Go into the Third Eye Meditation (see page 45) and visualize yourself filled with power (do not disperse it at the end of the meditation like usual). When you are ready, charge the candles to radiate spiritual energy and help you to connect to all things through body, mind, and heart. With the pin, scratch your desire for spirituality and the symbol of a knot (a basic pretzel shape is fine) on the candles.

Dress the candles with the spirituality oil. Next, light the incense while gazing at the statue or image of the chosen deity. Speak to the deity. Ask that they will guide you in your ways and that you will grow as a deeper, more spiritual person. When you feel filled with peace and spirituality, light the candles and chant:

> *Silver threads that bind us all,*
> *Move through me, break the wall.*
> *All forms of life, shall I see,*
> *Their inner essence and spirituality.*

Visualize silver threads reaching out from you in all directions and bringing you information from any being that you encounter. This information will be regarding that being's spiritual essence and will show you that all is one. We are all connected through the power of spirit. Each being in existence has its own destiny and role to fulfill as part of the greater macrocosm. Bury the remnants of this spell on a Monday, the day of the moon.

To Call an Animal Familiar

This spell is designed to draw an animal familiar to you. Before performing this rite, it is best to clearly decide on whatever physical, mental, and personality qualities you want the familiar to possess. Make a list of these attributes on a piece of paper and copy it down in your magical journal. Doing so will fine-tune your intent and ensure that the most "correct" familiar is drawn to you. Include on this list the type of animal you wish to have as your familiar. If you have no specific preference, simply ask for the animal familiar that is best suited to your life. Taking the time to clearly define the type of familiar you would like helps a proper match to be drawn to you. The more qualities and conditions you specify, the longer the spell can take. After all, calling for a familiar with certain qualities draws one to you; it doesn't make one for you. Be patient. This spell is best performed on the full moon.

Items needed:

- Beeswax or dark-brown candle (for the left)
- Beeswax or light-brown candle (for the right)
- List of desired attributes
- Picture or figurine of the type of familiar requested (if you have a preference)
- Cauldron or heat-proof bowl (to be used as a censer)
- Familiar oil (see page 206)
- Familiar incense (see page 206)
- Quick-lighting incense charcoal

Procedure

After you have gathered the ingredients and arranged your altar, you must take a cleansing bath. While bathing, contemplate all the practical factors involved in this spell such as how you will care for the familiar and all the attributes you want them to possess. The final step of preparation is to use one of the beginning meditations (such as the rainbow meditation) to bring you into a relaxed meditative state. It is now time to begin the spell.

First, it is necessary to summon energy, cast the circle, and light your altar candles. With the pin, scratch your desire into the brown candles and dress them with the oil as you pour energy and the loving desire to bond with an animal ally into the candles. Now, sit before the altar and light the charcoal in the cauldron. Sprinkle some of the burning mixture into the cauldron. As the scented smoke swirls, rises, and drifts through the air, study your list of attributes and visualize your ideal familiar; feel a deep emotional bond to the familiar.

When your energy, connection, and visualization are strong, light the candles (first left, then right) and chant the following spell:

For all good and by free will
Let my magic now fulfill.
Loving kinship now begin,
Ally, helper, guardian, friend.
Come to me, blessed spirit,
This bond now forged, may it never end.

Stare into the dark brown candle's flame as you focus on a "pulling" sense, creating a sort of energy current, a pathway for your familiar to reach you. As you do this, look once more at the list of attributes. Then light this list in the dark brown candle's flame and drop it into the cauldron. Say aloud to yourself, "It is done." Leave the candle burning for at least one hour (if it is safe to do so).

It is now necessary to ground your energy as you have been taught. After the candle is extinguished and has cooled, gather all the leftover bits from your spell and bury them in the earth. Then, of course, clean and put away your ritual tools.

To Remove Someone's Love for You

This spell will help you end an unwanted relationship or help quell the unwanted advances of an admirer.

Items needed:

- Beeswax or black candle (for the left)
- Beeswax or gray candle (for the right)
- Picture or personal item of the one to be removed
- Cauldron or heat-proof bowl (to be used as a censer)
- Go-away oil (see page 207)
- Go-away incense (see page 207)
- Pin

Procedure

First, take a cleansing bath and arrange the altar. Light the incense and go into a meditation. When you are relaxed, envision the one whose passions you wish to cool and see them slowly turn from their normal-colored self to black and white and then to gray. As you continue on, see them drift up and out of your life as if they were a dried leaf in autumn. When your visualization is strong, grasp the black and gray candles and charge them with a calm, un-aroused, bland, stale feeling of total disinterest. With the pin, carve your desire and an inverted pentagram into the wax (not for evil, see Symbolism section on page 56) and anoint them with the oil. Next, return the candles to the altar and pick up the photo or personal item. Focus on the item and feel your mind filling with complete rejection of the person whom it represents. When you are ready, light the candles left to right. In the flame of the black candle, ignite the photo or personal item and set it in the cauldron while chanting:

> *Your passion for me shall wither away,*
> *Removed from you, by light of day.*
> *Your ardent affection, unreturned,*
> *Out of my life, it shall be burned.*
> *By my will, for greater good,*
> *You are released; free and unbound.*

Visualize strongly and feel a peaceful existence without the person ever bothering you as though it has already occurred. Keep this visualization for as long as you can before opening the circle. Leave the candles burning (if it's safe to do so) for at least an hour, preferably until they extinguish on their own. Bury the remnants of the spell on a Wednesday, the day of communication.

Candle Making

It may be helpful to learn how to make your own candles for use in ritual. It is never a good idea to reuse candles from previous spells in new spells. Doing so would confuse the energy transmission and alter the spell. It is wise to melt down the globs of old wax and leftover candles from old spells and make some new candles to use. The fire and melting of the candle-making process releases any stored energy out of the wax; thus, purifying and readying it for use in new magic.

Items needed:

- Double boiler (to melt the wax)
- Heat-proof mold
- Beeswax
- Wick and pencil
- Oil (plain vegetable oil is preferred)
- Knife
- Spoon

Procedure

Coat the inside of the mold with a thin layer of the oil. I have used old pill bottles for candle molds, but you can find metal and silicone candle-making molds at arts-and-crafts stores. There is also special mold-release spray that helps to free the wax from the molds. Whatever your choice of candle molds, tie the wick to the pencil and set the wick inside the mold, laying the pencil on top of the mold to hold up the wick. Now, break up the beeswax into chunks and place in the double boiler. Since I don't have a double boiler, I have used a pot of boiling water with an old wok placed over the top and have had good results. Either way, be sure that you only use your double boiler for candle making. Boil the water first, then add the second piece holding the wax to melt it; stir continuously.

You may need to reheat the water occasionally, but I wouldn't leave the stove on the whole time. Steam burns hurt—this I know! When the wax has melted, wipe off the moisture from the bottom of the wok (or whatever) and then pour some wax three-fourths of the way up into the mold. Let the wax cool for at least an hour until a depression forms on the surface. When the wax has cooled, melt more wax in the double boiler and take the knife and break a hole in the depression in the candle. Slowly pour a little bit of wax in this hole to seal it and create a smooth surface. Let the candle cool overnight before pulling it out of the mold by the wick. It may be difficult to get the candle to release without breaking the mold; tapping the mold against a counter top helps.

After the candle has been freed from the mold, you may wish to smooth the outer surface of the candle. This can be done by boiling water in a large pot (to be used only for candle making), removing the pot from the heat, and very carefully dipping the candle into the water, holding it by the wick. This is must be done quickly; just dip in and pull out. The hot water melts the wax slightly and creates a beautiful smooth surface. After this, the candle can be charged for its purpose and used in magic. During the candle-making process, you could add herbs or oils into the wax of the candle in order to infuse it with the energies of those items, but this is a matter of preference.

Charms

Unlike casting a spell, where you send energy out toward a specific goal, a charm is an object (or group of objects) that is imbued with power for a specific goal. The power is then held within the charm to attract your goal to you or protect you from harm. A charm may either be a natural object such as a feather, crystal, or shell, or may be an object or objects specially constructed to work toward a goal. Charms to attract things or forces are known as talismans. Charms to deflect or repel people or forces for protective purposes are known as amulets.

Metals such as silver, gold, or iron should be used in the construction of amulets because metallic substances have natural deflection abilities. Organic materials such as wood, herbs, or shells should be used to make talismans as these substances have greater absorption and attraction capabilities. Crystals and stones carry traits of both metallic and organic matter so they may be used for amulets or talismans with equal success.

When creating a charm, all the ingredients of the charm must be symbolic of the desire sought. When charging the amulet or talisman (using the charging ritual on page 75), load it with energy and will that the intention stay in the object for as long as the object exists and that the charm will draw power from the cosmos as it is used. This will keep the charm from diminishing in strength as time passes.

The altar setup for the construction of a charm is usually the same as the basic altar setup used in spell casting. Sometimes, because we are not trying to expand and release energy outward but rather contain and intensify energy into a charm, a simpler altar with only a censer, a cauldron, the charm ingredients, and a few other objects may be used to keep the power close. As in all things magical, variations and personal adjustments are encouraged to suit your own taste.

Astrological Talisman

Even those with little to no knowledge or interest in the power of astrology usually know their sign. Each zodiac sign is believed to carry certain personality traits that can manifest in either positive or negative ways. A brief list includes:

Aries (March 21–April 21): red; ruled by Mars; daring and impatient, strong and dominating

Taurus (April 22–May 21): green; ruled by Venus; level-headed and stubborn, decisive and overbearing

Gemini (May 22–June 21): orange; ruled by Mercury; communicative and babbling, friendly and scattered

Cancer (June 22–July 21): silver; ruled by the moon; nurturing and smothering, sensitive and melancholy

Leo (July 22–August 22): gold; ruled by the sun; outgoing and obnoxious, optimistic and deluded

Virgo (August 23–September 21): yellow; ruled by Mercury; organized and nitpicky, cerebral and mercurial

Libra (September 22–October 21): pink; ruled by Venus; friendly and insincere, helpful and indecisive

Scorpio (October 22-November 21): black; ruled by Pluto; independent and detached, original and secretive

Sagittarius (November 22–December 21): royal blue; ruled by Jupiter; fun-loving and noncommittal, free thinking and impractical

Capricorn (December 22–January 20): indigo; ruled by Saturn; hard-working and boring, practical and stodgy

Aquarius (January 21–February 19): white; ruled by Uranus; social and aloof, humanitarian and gullible

Pisces (February 20–March 20): opalescent blue; ruled by Neptune; sensitive and erratic, imaginative and unrealistic

Zodiac Charm

A specific charm can be created for a person in their astrological sign to channel the positive aspects of that sign and minimize the sign's negative aspects.

Items needed:

- Disk of wood (no greater than three inches in diameter)
- Paint (in astrological color) or carving tool
- Cauldron
- Candle in astrological color
- Zodiac incense for your sign (see page 220)
- Censer
- Quick-lighting incense charcoal

Procedure

To create this charm first, obtain a small disk of wood. On this disk, paint or carve the astrological symbol for your sign on one side and the symbol of its planetary ruler (see Symbolism, page 56) on the other side. Next, properly prepare with a cleansing bath. Now, set up your altar with a single candle in the appropriate color for your sign placed within the cauldron. Place the cauldron in the middle of the altar table and set the censer behind it; place the disk of wood and other charm ingredients in front of the cauldron, perhaps on a pentacle if desired. Finally, cast a circle. Then, go into a meditation. When you are relaxed, focus on the positive qualities of your zodiac sign and fill yourself with these qualities. Feel happy and content. When this state is achieved, pick up the disk and infuse it with this positive energy; visualize this energy as light in the color of your zodiac sign pouring into the charm from your third eye and hands, willing that it remain in the disk for as long as the disk exists and that it will draw in further energy from your ruling planet in order to reinforce the positive aspects of your sign. Finally, pass the charm through the smoke of the incense and say:

> *May the positive qualities locked*
> *within be unleashed for all to see,*
> *And as I will, so shall it be.*

Wear the charm as much as you can (hidden on you, if possible) in order to absorb its influence.

Healing Charm

A charm can be made to feed healing energy to the body to aid in recovery from illness or injury. In creating this charm, it is a good idea to put as much of yourself into it as possible. The true beginning of any magical process is when you decide what you are going to do and begin gathering the ingredients. If you take the time to connect with the process of constructing any charm, particularly one as important as a healing charm, its power will be greatly enhanced. Cut the wood yourself, paint or carve it yourself, etc. if possible. It is good to use oak wood for this charm because the oak is sacred and will empower you with its strength. If you choose to paint the symbols on the wood, blue paint should be used.

Items needed:

- Wooden disk (no greater than three inches in diameter)
- Healing oil (see page 208)
- Healing incense (see page 207)
- Blue candle (for the left)
- Red candle (for the right)
- Censer
- Paint or carving tool
- Pentacle (or plate)

Procedure

This rite is best performed during the waxing or full moon. Before anything else, you must cut a branch of wood and then cut off as thin a circle of wood as you can from the cut branch. Next, sand the disc smooth and carve, paint, or engrave a solar cross (a cross inside a circle) on one side of the disc and a triangle on the other side. The cross symbolizes the creation of a nexus point (a point through which energy flows) and the circle surrounding it symbolizes the containment of this energy so that you may use it. The triangle symbolizes vitalizing growth energy, which is the energy type we are trying to draw and channel.

First, cast the circle and place the disc on the pentacle or plate. Then, take a magical cleansing bath and arrange your altar according to the basic altar setup. The blue candle and red candle are anointed with healing oil; the healing incense should be smoldering.

Light the candles and go into a meditation. Visualize yourself (or another) in a completely healthy, strong state. Once you have completed the meditation, draw in pure healing energy (bright blue light) from the universe and visualize the disc being a powerfully charged talisman for as long as it exists. Now, open your eyes and pick up the charm. Holding it in your right hand, will your own energy and the universal energy that you've gathered into the talisman. At the same time, focus on how you want to feel (or how you want the wearer to feel) while the talisman is on your body (healthy, strong, happy, etc.).

When you have filled the talisman with as much energy as you can, will that it shall draw in further energy from the universe as needed in order to maintain its charge. Finally, hold it briefly over the flame of the red candle (carefully!), then anoint the charm with a drop of healing oil. Hold it in the smoke of the incense while chanting:

Vital strength fills this charm,
Healing to its wearer impart.
Perfect health is now restored,
Health to the body, strength to the heart!

The talisman is now charged and complete. Proclaim, "For the good of all, this charm is made," and open the circle. Keep the talisman with you whenever possible to absorb its healing energies.

Love Charm

This is an old love charm. The charm consists of snail shells strung together on a red or pink thread, either to be worn as a necklace or hung in the home. Personally, I'd go with the hang-it-up-in-the-house option but either way will work. Snails are associated with love and sexuality, so you can use their shells to create an aura of love energy around you. The trick is to find twelve intact snail shells; twelve is a magical number relating to the twelve zodiac signs and the months of the calendar year. Do not kill any snails for this charm. The snails must vacate the shells on their own (however that may be), or the charm's effect will be altered. Just be on the lookout for empty snail shells in your yard or whatever until you have acquired twelve. You will also need pink or red thread and a sturdy needle.

Being a practical person, I prefer to do all the tedious tasks in the charm-making process before actually lighting candles and working the ritual. Mistakes happen, and like many, I have a tendency to swear when I accidentally jab my finger with a needle; doing so while empowering the charm in the circle would disrupt the intention and scatter the power. I would advise that you string the shells on the thread before you prepare the charging rite. To string the shells, thread your needle with a long enough thread to easily fit over your head. Next, tie a small knot at the open end of the thread about three inches up (not at the very end). Carefully poke the needle through one snail shell. Only make one hole in the shell. Don't try to stab it through the middle to make them perfectly placed symmetrical beads; this is difficult to do perfectly, and the shells will likely break. Once you have the shell on the thread, gently slide it down to the knot toward the end of the thread. Now, tie another knot in the thread so that there is a knot on each side of the shell. Repeat this process with each of the remaining shells; string, slide, and knot until all twelve shells are strung. The final knot should be tied to loop the shells together like a necklace. There should be a total of thirteen knots.

Items needed:

- Beeswax or red candle for the opposite sex, beeswax or purple for same-sex (for the left)
- Beeswax or pink candle for the opposite sex, beeswax or lavender for same-sex (for the right)
- Love oil (see pages 208-209)
- Cauldron or heat-proof bowl (to be used as a censer)
- Love incense (see pages 208-209)
- Quick-lighting charcoal
- 1 cup saltwater
- Stone, plate, or pentacle

Procedure

Ritually bathe and cast your circle as usual. Place the shell necklace on the stone, plate, or pentacle. Go into a meditation. When you are relaxed, visualize yourself holding the shell necklace and being surrounded by a bright-pink aura of light. Feel this aura having a magnetic quality to it; feel that it will attract like-minded individuals to you by its very presence. Visualize this as strongly as you can. When you feel you are ready, pick up the necklace and infuse this image and energy into the necklace through the power of your will. Imagine the pink light streaming out of your hands and into the necklace. See it absorbed into each shell and into each knot, your will becoming linked and forever bound to this object. See the light radiating out of the necklace, glowing with magical force.

It is now time to consecrate the charm in the name of your patron or favorite "love" deity. Anoint the necklace with love oil and then place it again on the stone, plate, or pentacle. Sprinkle it with saltwater; pick it up and pass it through the incense smoke and over the flame of the right (beeswax, pink, or lavender) candle. Finally, cup the necklace in both hands and breathe loving energy into it while chanting:

> *Through earth and water, air and fire*
> *Cleansed and charged with my desire.*
> *Shells of snail, knotted cord,*
> *Draw the correct love to me,*
> *With passionate force.*

The charm is now complete. Open the circle and either hang the charm in your bedroom or wear it often to surround yourself with an attractive aura of love energy.

Charm for Employment

A metal key can be used as a charm to "unlock" new opportunities for a new job. You will need to obtain a metal key, preferably of the traditional old-fashioned skeleton-key type; in a pinch, any key can be used. If you use a regular key, make sure that it is either a new blank key or a properly cleansed (in blessed saltwater) key for which you no longer have a current use.

Items needed:

- Metal key
- Blue candle to draw in Jupiter's energy (for the left)
- Green candle to release the energy of abundance (for the right)
- Cauldron or heat-proof bowl to be used as a censer
- Luck oil (see page 210)
- Money oil (see page 211)
- Luck incense (see page 210)
- Cord (black, green, or gold)

Procedure

This charm is best created during a waxing moon and on a Thursday. First, take a magical cleansing bath. Then, arrange your altar according to the basic steps and cast a circle. Light the incense; anoint the blue candle with luck oil and the green candle with money oil. Light the candles and pick up the key. Go into your meditation. When you are relaxed, visualize the type of job that you are seeking (not a specific job). See yourself working at the type of job that you wish; feel satisfied and content to be there. See the key unlocking the door to your new place of business. Infuse this energy into the key and will that it shall stay within the key. As you charge the key, chant the following words three, seven, or nine times:

Magic key, unlock for me the job that I seek!

Now, string the key on the cord; wear it as a pendant when you are looking for work and to all interviews (under your clothes). When not in use, store the charm in a blue or green natural-fiber bag for safekeeping.

Key Charm for a New Home

A key is the perfect charm for seeking a new home. If you use one of your old keys for this charm, make sure that it is thoroughly cleansed in saltwater. Ensure that it was not the key to a previous home (this could confuse the intent of the spell).

Items needed:
- Metal key
- Brown candle for earth energy (for the left)
- Green candle for growth and abundance (for the right)

- Cauldron or heat-proof bowl to
  be used as a censer
- Luck oil (see page 210)
- Luck incense (see page 210)
- Cord (white, brown, or green)

Procedure

This charm is best created during a waxing moon. First, take a magical cleansing bath. When you are finished, anoint your forehead, wrists, and back of the neck with luck oil. Arrange the altar and cast your circle. Anoint the candles with the oil and light the incense. Pick up the key and go into your meditation. When you are ready, visualize the type of home you wish to have; focus on a relaxed, safe, peaceful feeling at this home you are envisioning. Infuse this feeling and energy into the key while you chant the following:

> *Power of earth, heed my call;*
> *Charge this key to open the door.*
> *With harm to none, for good of all*
> *Bring the home I'm searching for.*

Now, string the key onto the cord and wear it as often as possible, especially when you search for your new home.

Charm of Good Fortune

Luck charms are often misunderstood, as is the general nature of luck. Luck is both the ability and circumstance of making the "correct" decision at the necessary time. For example, if you decide to go to the store early, say at 5:00 p.m. instead of 5:30 p.m., and in so doing you have unknowingly avoided a horrible accident, then you would be perceived as lucky. If you thought about going early but were too tired, and got into a horrible accident as a result of leaving later, then you would of course be considered unlucky. Luck is really a matter of connecting to (and listening to) your intuition and higher consciousness.

In creating a luck charm, what you create is a charm designed to aid your ability to make choices that will result in positive actions and consequences in your life. It is much like making a charm to increase psychic ability in that it will help you communicate in a greater way with your own inner guidance. The following charm is quite old and time tested. If properly made, it should serve you well. This spell is best done on a Thursday, Jupiter's day, during a waxing moon.

Items needed:

- Horseshoe or horseshoe trinket
- Hair or nail clippings from yourself
- Cauldron or heat-proof bowl
  to be used as a censer
- Luck oil (see page 210)
- Luck incense (see page 210)
- Royal blue candle to draw in Jupiter's
  energy (for the left)
- Light green candle for luck (for the right)
- Royal blue natural-fiber bag to hold
  the horseshoe

Procedure

First, take a magical cleansing bath. Afterward, anoint your forehead with luck oil. Cast the circle. Light the luck incense; anoint the candles with the oil and light the candles (blue first, then green). Go into a meditation. When you are ready, focus on a peaceful feeling and visualize yourself having the best possible day, a day when everything goes your way. Feel blissful and content. When you feel at the peak of happiness and luck, call on the energy of the planet Jupiter and ask that good-luck energy fills you with every breath you take. Breathe in the energy of Jupiter and pick up the horseshoe. Will this energy into the horseshoe and state that it will stay in the horseshoe for as long as the horseshoe exists and that the Jupiter energy will renew itself as time goes by. Next, place the horseshoe in the royal blue bag along with your hair or nail clippings. Bury the bag in the ground, preferably at a crossroads.

Money Charm

To create a charm to draw money, take either two new silver coins or two coins that were minted in the year of your birth. Charge them using the method that follows.

Items needed:

- 2 coins
- Beeswax or green candle to draw in growth (for the left)
- Beeswax or gold candle to unleash the energy of abundance (for the right)

- Royal blue candle placed before the cauldron to bring in Jupiter's influence (optional)
- Money oil (see page 211)
- Money incense (see page 210)
- Cauldron or heat-proof bowl (to be used as a censer)

Procedure

First, take a cleansing bath and cast a circle. Light the incense in the cauldron and dress the candles with the money oil. Anoint your wrists, third eye, and the back of your neck with the money oil. Light the candles left to right and watch them glow for a minute. Go into a meditation. When you are relaxed, focus on a feeling of relaxed security and visualize having the amount of money that you need. As you focus in your meditation, draw in power from the earth; visualize this power as pure gold light for abundance. When you feel that the power is at its peak, open your eyes and pick up the coins. Pour the money energy into the coins while chanting:

Money magic fills the charms,
For good of all and without harm.
Linked together, the coins shall bring
Abundance and prosperity.

To use these charms, one coin should be placed in your wallet or purse (be sure to keep it in a special place so that you don't accidentally spend it) and the other coin should be buried in the earth (preferably at a crossroads during a waxing moon on Jupiter's day, Thursday).

Pendulum

Any object can be made into a pendulum. A pendulum is a device where an object acts as a weight attached to a chain or cord. You hold the pendulum by the cord and ask a yes or no question. The weight will begin to swing in either a back-and-forth or a circular motion. This movement will indicate the answer to your question.

Perhaps the best medium to use as a pendulum is a quartz crystal on a natural fiber cord. Purple or black would be good colors for the cord. Quartz has inherent electrical properties that help it react when used as a pendulum. After you have either made or purchased your pendulum, you should consecrate it before its first use and dedicate it to the purpose of divination.

Items needed:
- Pendulum
- 2 tablespoons mugwort or white rose petals
- 1½ cups water (for tea)
- Cauldron
- Psychic incense (see page 214)
- Black candle (for the left)
- White candle (for the right)

Procedure
To consecrate the pendulum, on the first night of the full moon brew a tea made from mugwort or white rose petals in your cauldron and allow it to cool. When it has cooled, take the cauldron to your altar and have psychic incense and the black and white candles burning. Next, dip the crystal

into the brew and then waft it in the smoke of the incense and carefully pass it over the flames of both candles, left then right. Finally, cup the crystal in both hands and gently breathe your energy into it while chanting:

> *Cleansed and charged, your magic pure,*
> *Through each realm your powers shine.*
> *Spirit connection, now secure,*
> *To bring the truths, I divine.*

The pendulum is now ready for your questions to begin. To discover which motion means yes and which means no, simply ask your pendulum an obvious yes answer and then ask it an obvious no answer; pay attention to the ways in which the pendulum swings these two times. You may wish to do this several times at first if the movements seem unclear. Keep the pendulum in a purple or black bag made of natural fibers when not in use. Using a pendulum may take several attempts before you get the hang of it but it is a worthy pursuit as it will lead to your enhanced understanding. As long as you are the only one to hold the pendulum, it should not need to be consecrated again. Others may ask questions, but you should hold it.

Charm for Increased Magical Power

This charm is worn on the body to enhance your innate ability to draw in spiritual energy; it will also help you develop your mental and psychic faculties.

Items needed:

- Equal parts of rose, mugwort, thyme, and mint
- Square of purple cloth
- Purple cord or ribbon
- Power oil (see page 212)
- Power incense (see page 212)
- Purple candle

Procedure

This charm is best created during the full moon. First, gather your ingredients and take a cleansing bath. Cast your circle, anoint the purple candle with power oil, and light both the candle and the power incense. Mix the herbs together in a bowl and go into a meditation. When you are relaxed, visualize yourself brimming with power, surrounded by a huge aura of white light, a glow of yellow-gold light in the area of your forehead (third eye), a glow of blue-green light in the area of your heart, and a red glow in the area of your groin. See all the light merge into a purple light. Concentrate the light into your hands, open your eyes, and place your hands over the bowl of herbs. Concentrate on sending the energy into the herbs, charging them with power. Sprinkle the herbs into the center of the purple bag and bring the corners together, trapping the charged herbs inside. Now take the purple cord and wind it around the gathered corners to seal the bag. Now tie nine knots in the cord and chant:

> *Magic charm, build my will,*
> *Lend me strength, hour by hour.*
> *To my mind and heart, please fill,*
> *Open me to the spirit power.*

Carry the bag with you as often as possible. Sleep with it under your pillow and rub it over your third eye before meditations and magical ritual.

Malice Stones

This talisman can be a cleansing and therapeutic tool to rid you of negativity. To create a malice stone is to create a battery of negativity and anger outside of ourselves so that we may be free of such stress. It can be charged whenever necessary. Always return the stone to its spell box for safekeeping so that its energy can be contained. If it is not contained, it will radiate negativity wherever it sits. For instructions on how to create spell boxes, see Chapter 10.

Items needed:
- Smooth stone that will fit in one hand
- Cleansed and blessed spell box to store the stone

Procedure
Whenever you are filled with anger, simply hold the stone in your hand and grasp it in a fist. Feel the angry energy transfer into the stone and will that it shall remain locked within the stone until you release it. After you have released your anger into the stone, place the stone in the spell box to contain its energy and prevent anyone from coming into contact with its negativity. This procedure may be repeated over and over again as a way of releasing hate and anger from your body and spirit.

Personal Amulet

Objects can be charged to offer personal protection in times of need and for general protection against disturbing energies and forces. Amulets ideally should be in the form of jewelry or garments since these may be easily and inconspicuously worn for long periods of time. The form chosen for an amulet should be one that can be worn over or near a person's primary receptive psychic center. In some people this will be the third eye while in others it could be the heart area, the hands, the solar plexus, etc. Different people have sensitivity in different places. Generally speaking, your primary psychic center will be known to you because this will be the area that will become warm, tingling, tense, or upset when impressions or warnings come upon you.

If your psychic center is in your hands, a ring or bracelet should be chosen for an amulet. If your psychic center is your heart, a pendent should be used for an amulet, etc. Use your best judgment. The object chosen should contain some type of protective stone, metal, color, or symbolism; this helps the object to retain the protective charge.

Items needed:
- Object chosen to be the amulet
- Protection oil (see page 213)
- Protection incense (see page 212)
- Blessed saltwater
- Pentacle or plate
- Black candle (for the left)
- Red candle (for the right)

Procedure

This rite is best performed during the waxing or full moon. First, take a magical cleansing bath, then arrange your altar according to the basic altar setup, using the black candle on the left and the red candle on the right. Both candles should be anointed with protection oil. Light the incense (it should be smoldering for the charm). Cast the circle and place the amulet on the pentacle or plate. Light the candles and anoint the amulet with blessed saltwater and state that any incorrect energies are cast out and that only positive protective energy shall be held within this amulet. Sit before the altar and go into a meditation (the three cauldron meditation works well for this). Once you have completed the meditation, draw in pure protection energy (bright white light) from the universe and visualize that your amulet will be powerfully charged for as long as it exists. Now, open your eyes and pick up the amulet. Holding it in your right hand, will your own energy and the universal energy that you've gathered into the amulet. Mentally pour energy into the amulet; at the same time, focus on how you want to feel while wearing it (safe, secure, relieved, content, etc.).

When you have filled the amulet with as much energy as you can, will that it shall draw in further energy from the universe as needed in order to maintain the magical charge. Finally, hold the amulet briefly over the flame of the red candle (carefully!), anoint it with a drop of protection oil, and hold it in the smoke of the incense declaring:

A charm of protection, now and forever
Charged by land, by sky, and by sea,

Blessed with oil, flame, smoke, and water
As I will, so shall it be!

The amulet is now charged and complete. Open the circle and then wear the amulet. Store it in a safe place until needed, or give the amulet to the one to be protected.

Warding

Warding is the act of creating protective amulets and placing them evenly around the area to be protected (such as a home or car) in order to keep out unwanted forces. Warding can be done with quartz crystals or flat metal discs painted with a protective symbol (such as a solar cross within a circle).

The individual amulets are charged and linked together so that their combined power will create an interlaced network of threads around the property to deflect negativity. In the case of protecting a house, a ward will need to be placed in each window and over any entrance into the home. If a single room is to be protected, a ward should be placed in each corner of the room. If a plot of land is to be protected, then enough amulets to encircle the entire property will have to be made. The amulets should be placed no more than ten feet apart. In this case, the amulets may be buried around the property.

Items needed:
- Objects chosen to be wards (amulets)
- Warding incense (see page 213)
- Cauldron or heat-proof bowl
- Beeswax or white candle

- Protection oil (see page 213)
- Incense charcoal
- Censer

Procedure

This rite is best performed during the waxing or full moon. To create the wards, first you will need to determine how many you will need and obtain as many crystals or metal discs as necessary. Next, if metal discs were chosen, they must be painted with a proper symbol using white paint (see Symbolism on page 56). Then, whether crystals or discs, they must be gathered together in the cauldron or a large bowl to be charged.

Prepare the mixture of warding incense. Please note that the warding incense contains toxic ingredients, so only burn the incense in small amounts with proper ventilation and be sure to keep any magical mixtures away from pets or children. Place the cauldron with the wards and the unlit white or beeswax candle on the altar. Now you must prepare yourself for the magic by bathing in blessed saltwater and focusing on the intention that, once linked together and put in place, the wards will create a sphere of protective energy that will envelop the area. At the same time, build within yourself the contented feeling of being protected. Feel as if the work has already been completed and security is guaranteed and absolute.

Now cast a circle and anoint the candle with the protection oil. Light the candle and the incense as you sit (or stand) before the cauldron of wards. Summon power and ask your patron deity (if you have one) to charge these amulets with protective power. Place your hands over the cauldron and send your power into them while visualizing that as each amulet absorbs power, it joins with the others like links in a chain. As you pour energy into the wards, chant the following spell:

Guardian force, protect this space,
Threads of magic, shield this land,
Merge your power, weave the web,
Gifts from earth join hand in hand.

After you have completed the charging, will that the wards shall draw in the universal light continuously for as long as they exist in order to renew themselves and keep their power strong. Place the wards in their designated locations as soon as possible.

five

Crystal and Gem Magic

C rystals and gemstones have been utilized in magic and ritual for many centuries. In fact, most of the customs relating to modern use of stones as jewelry and decoration originate from their use as magical talismans. Wearing a gemstone in a ring, for example, helps the stone transmit its energy and properties to the person wearing it. In modern times, most New Age people, and some of us "old agers" as I like to say, utilize crystals as a means of building and transmitting magical power. Quartz in particular has remarkable properties (such as the ability to conduct electricity) and is used for a variety of purposes in both the magical and scientific arenas.

Anyone can tap into the power of stones and crystals. It must be understood that crystals and stones are considered to be a form of life (because they grow and exchange energy) and should be respected as such. View them as a type of ally, much like a familiar possession as opposed to an inert possession. All forms of natural matter carry life energies and should therefore be treated with care and respect.

In my tradition, we place high value on the colors of stones because different colors transmit in different frequency ranges. Any stone of a certain color carries similar properties as another stone of the same color.

Crystals and Gems by Color

White: milky quartz, moonstone

Pink: rose quartz, pink tourmaline

Red: ruby, garnet, red jasper

Orange: carnelian, fire opal

Yellow: citrine, amber, topaz, golden calcite, yellow jasper

Green: jade, emerald, peridot, aventurine, malachite

Blue: sapphire, lapis lazuli, topaz, aquamarine, sodalite

Indigo: dark amethyst, dark tanzanite, iolite, sugilite, charoite

Violet: amethyst, agate, spinel

Brown: tiger's eye, petrified wood, jasper, brown chalcedony, brown agate

Black: obsidian, onyx (for Capricorns only; it tends to scatter other signs' energy), hematite, jet

Multicolored stones: ametrine, snowflake obsidian, alexandrite, fluorite, bloodstone, many types of jasper and jade.

Crystals and Gems by Abilities

Amethyst: Amethyst helps the mind and psychic abilities, brings luck, and minimizes the effect of drunkenness.

Clear quartz: Clear quartz is a multipurpose stone and amplifies magical energy. It helps to diffuse excess electrical energy in the body, and so can be used to bring calm.

Emerald: Emerald is used to uncover psychic abilities and past lives.

Garnet: Garnet is useful for love magic.

Hematite: Hematite is a grounding stone used to leach out any negativity.

Jade: Jade is a stone of healing and balancing.

Lodestone: This natural magnet is usually used in pairs to aid in attracting your goals.

Moonstone: This stone enhances psychic ability and the ability to connect to the feminine half of divinity.

Multicolored stones: These stones carry energies indicated by each of the colors present in the stone as well as Uranus energy.

Obsidian: This is another grounding and protective stone; it should be charged and worn any time you are around negative, draining people.

Rose quartz: This is an aid to love magic as well as a balancer of emotions.

Ruby: Ruby is power enhancing and helps to focus spiritual energy.

Sapphire: Sapphire helps in uncovering truth and is protective.

Tiger's eye: This is a protective stone that is also used to enhance success.

There are many different ways to use crystals and gems in magic. The first and simplest method is through the wearing of jewelry. If you have a favorite ring, pendant, or bracelet that has a useful stone, just charge the jewelry to be a talisman in accordance with your desire and the inherent properties of the stone. For example, I have an amethyst ring that was a gift from my mother. I wanted to enhance my psychic ability, so I charged the amethyst to be a talisman of psychic energy (as it is violet in color and has the quality of enhancing psychic power).

Charging a Crystal or Gem

To simply charge a crystal or gem, first go into a meditation while holding the stone (or placing your hands on it if it's too large to hold). When you are relaxed, visualize the stone and "see" the aura around it with your third eye. Whatever you initially see, gradually visualize it changing and growing in brightness, shifting to a strong energy the same color as the stone. This will remove any negative or unfocused energies attached to the stone. When you have this image strong in your mind, fill your mind with your magical goal and infuse the stone with this goal. See it as power streaming from your hands and third eye into the stone. Finally, visualize all the power being absorbed into the stone and will that it shall stay there for as long as you need it to stay (either for a moon cycle, a year, or a lifetime, whatever you decide is appropriate to the future use of the stone), then conclude your meditation and open your eyes.

In addition to using a crystal or gem on its own, another method of utilizing stones in magic is to add them to other forms of magic. In a candle spell, boost the energy sent forth by placing one or several crystals or gems that are in line with your goal on the altar in rings around the candles. If you are making a charm bag, add one or several appropriate crystals or gems to the other ingredients in the bag to increase its power. Similarly, you can add crystals or gems to witch bottles, place them in the jars of oil, stuff them into poppets, etc. Use your creativity to find new uses for crystals and gems.

Witch Bottles

A witch bottle is a special type of charm originally only used to draw and contain or neutralize evil forces. In modern times, the uses of witch bottles have been expanded to aid in the achievement of a variety of other goals. To start, you will need a small glass bottle with a cork stopper and either a beeswax or appropriately colored candle.

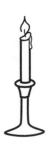

There are two types of protective witch bottles: the traditional and the modern. The traditional version does contain some unsavory ingredients, so the modern witch bottle may be preferred by some. Both versions will be effective.

Traditional Protective Witch Bottle

This bottle is designed to absorb and neutralize negativity and curses being sent your way. Your personal items are used, in effect, to "fool" the energy of a curse into attacking the witch bottle instead of you. The other items in the bottle are used to break up and neutralize the curse. These types of bottles have been in use for over five hundred years and are a strong means of protection and curse removal. This bottle is best made during the waning moon.

Items needed:

- Green, blue, or black glass bottle (three to six inches in height) and a cork stopper
- 2 chicken bones from a black hen or chicken feathers (optional)

- 9 or more bent nails or pins (preferably rusty and old)
- 9 or more thorns from a blackthorn bush
- Beeswax or black candle
- 3 black cords (nine inches in length; natural fiber preferred)
- Lock of your hair
- Sample of your urine (enough to fill the bottle)

Procedure

Before performing the spell, you must take the ritual bath, then arrange the altar and cast the circle. Then, each item must be charged separately. The bottle is charged first; it is charged with the intent that it will be a beacon for any negative energy sent to you. Next, the chicken bones or feathers are charged with the ability to absorb the negative energy. The bent pins or nails are then charged to puncture through and weaken any negativity sent your way. Next, the thorns are charged to neutralize and remove the harmful intentions contained in the energy of the curse. The candle is also charged with the ability to dissolve and neutralize the negativity. Finally, the cords are the last items to be charged. The hair and urine will not be charged since their purpose is only to carry your energy (and already do). The cord charging will begin the ritual to empower the witch bottle.

Before charging the cords, make sure that all the other ingredients are charged and gathered together. Now, settle before the altar in quiet meditation. Use one of the meditations previously given first and move into a visualization of what you want the bottle to accomplish. See the dark energies and forces being absorbed into the bottle and then being trapped, shredded, and dissolved within it.

After your visualization, light the black candle and pick up all three of the cords and tie them together in a large knot at one end. See this knot as binding the force of your spell. Hold this knot between your teeth and slowly begin to braid the cords together. While you braid, continue to focus on the intent of the bottle and bind this intent into your cord. When you have braided about halfway down, tie a second knot into the three cords. Again, see this knot as binding in the intentions of your spell. Continue to braid the cords together until you reach the end, where a final knot shall be tied. The three cords should now be one braided piece with three knots total. As you tie this final knot, be convinced that any negative energy sent your way shall be drawn into and trapped in the witch bottle.

Now, place the completed cord in the bottle, along with the thorns, nails, bones or feathers, and lock of your hair. Next, pour in the urine and securely cork the bottle. With the cork in place, pour melted wax from the black candle over the cork to permanently seal the bottle and activate the spell. As your pour the wax say:

> Witch's bottle, protect me from harm sent my way;
> Shred harm's power both night and day.

Once the cork has been completely covered and the bottle sealed, end the rite and open the circle. Take the bottle outside and bury it under your home, at the farthest point on your property, or beneath the bricks of the fireplace.

These are the traditional areas in which to bury the bottle and keep the negativity away from you. It is done.

Modern Protective Witch Bottle

This bottle is designed to work similarly to the traditional bottle but with more pleasant ingredients. The saliva replaces the urine. The recipe for the brew can be found in Chapter 14. The brew is used to replace both the physical volume of the urine and the magical function of the black cords. The brew will bind the spell.

Items needed:
- Green, blue, or black glass bottle (three to six inches in height) and a cork stopper
- 9 or more bent, rusty nails
- Broken glass or junk plastic
- Saliva
- Lock of hair
- Modern protective witch bottle brew (cooled)
- Black candle

Procedure

You must first make the brew and allow it to cool. While it is cooling, take a cleansing bath. When the brew has cooled, take it into your ritual area and arrange your altar. Place the bottle and personal items on the left, the nails and broken glass in bowls on the right, and the black candle and brew in the middle. Now, cast your circle. When all is ready, charge the bottle to attract any negativity sent in your direction. Next, charge the nails and broken glass to shred and neutralize the negative energy. After that, charge the candle with the ability to neutralize negativity. Finally, the brew is charged to bind and contain the energy so that it cannot escape.

After this charging, light the black candle, settle yourself before the altar, and go into a meditation. After you are relaxed, begin a visualization of your intended goal for the bottle. See the negative energies being absorbed into the bottle and then being shredded, neutralized, and forever trapped. Truly feel relieved, safe, and protected. After the visualization, begin to fill the bottle. Start with the lock of your hair. Then add the nails and broken glass. Next, add the saliva (usually by simply spitting into the bottle). Finally, slowly pour in the brew. As you pour the brew into the bottle, say:

> *Curses, hexes, ill will, unwound;*
> *In the bottle, forever be bound!*

Once the bottle has been filled, securely cork it and pour melted wax from the black candle over the cork to permanently seal it. As is the case with the traditional witch bottle, bury this bottle at the farthest point on your property, under the house, or under the bricks of the hearth. Or, if you live in an apartment, hide it where no one will find it. It is done.

Health Bottle

This witch bottle is designed to ensure continued good health (as opposed to healing of illness).

Items needed:
- Green or brown glass bottle with tight-fitting lid or cork

- 1 tablespoon thyme leaves
- 5 willow leaves
- 1 tablespoon of rose petals
- 1 tablespoon of shredded pine needles
- Lock of your own hair or nail clippings
- Spring water (enough to fill the bottle)
- Green candle

Procedure

Gather the ingredients, take a cleansing bath, arrange the altar, and cast the circle. When you are ready, charge the herbs to bring you continued good health for as long as the bottle remains sealed. After this charging, light the green candle, settle yourself before the altar, and go into a meditation. After you are relaxed, begin a visualization of your intended goal for the bottle. See yourself in a strong, healthy state of being, free from any ills. Truly feel healthy, happy, and strong. After the visualization, begin filling the bottle. First, place your hair or nail clippings into the bottle. Next, add the herbs. Add the spring water last. Tightly cork the bottle and then drip wax from the green candle on the cork (or lid) to seal it and bind your spell. Chant:

> *Healthy body, healthy mind,*
> *Strength in me, I shall find,*
> *Robust health, ever mine,*
> *Bottle sealed, for all time.*

The bottle should then be placed in some secret location or buried in the ground, perhaps beneath a healthy plant or tree. It is done.

Love Bottle

This bottle shall draw love energy to you, thus making you more loving and at the same time more attractive to others.

Items needed:
- Pink or red glass bottle
- 1 tablespoon rose petals
- 1 tablespoon chamomile
- 1 tablespoon catnip
- 1 tablespoon yarrow
- Lock of your own hair or fingernail clippings
- Apple juice or cider (enough to fill the bottle)
- Pink candle

Procedure

Arrange the altar and cast the circle. When you are ready, charge the herbs to bring loving energy your way for as long as the bottle remains sealed. After this charging, light the pink candle, settle yourself before the altar, and go into a meditation. After you are relaxed, begin a visualization of your intended goal for the bottle; see and feel yourself as peaceful, happy, and loved, surrounded by loved ones and friends. Visualize a general image of your ideal mate. Truly *feel* happy, peaceful, and loved. After the visualization, begin filling the bottle. First, add your hair or nail clippings. Next, add the herbs. Finish by adding enough apple juice to fill up the bottle completely. Tightly cork the bottle and then drip wax from the pink candle on the cork (or lid) to seal it and bind your spell. Chant:

Power of love, fill me now,
Bring to me my heart's true mate.
Without harm, by free will I vow,
Forged in joy; sealed in fate.

Place the bottle in your bedroom where you can see it often but where it won't be disturbed by others. It is done.

Luck Bottle

Nothing is more irritating than a streak of bad luck. This bottle helps ensure that you make the right choices and are at the right place at the right time in order to avoid those unpleasant setbacks.

Items needed:
- Royal blue bottle
- Hair or nail clippings
- 1 tablespoon cinquefoil
- 1 tablespoon mistletoe
- 1 tablespoon dandelion
- 1 tablespoon clover
- 1 tablespoon thyme
- Spring water (to fill the bottle)
- Blue candle (for Jupiter)
- Pin

Procedure

Arrange the altar and cast the circle. When you are ready, charge the herbs to bring good fortune into your life for as long as the bottle remains sealed. Then, carve the Jupiter symbol on the blue candle to bring the influence of Jupiter to your spell; charge the candle with the energy of Jupiter. After this charging, light the blue candle, settle yourself before the altar, and go into a meditation. After you are relaxed, begin a visualization of your intended goal for the bottle; see and feel yourself as lucky, happy, and successful. After the visualization, begin filling the bottle. First add your hair or nail clippings. Next, add the herbs. Finish with the spring water. Tightly cork the bottle and drip wax from the blue candle on the cork (or lid) to seal it and bind your spell. Chant:

Jupiter smile down on me,
Bring good fortune to my life.
Filled with luck, I am free,
Of mistakes, trauma, and strife.

Place the bottle somewhere that you will be able to see it often but where it won't be disturbed by others. It is done.

Money Bottle

This bottle will generate a force of success around you that will attract situations and people to create more money in your life.

Items needed:
- Lock of hair or nail clippings
- 1 tablespoon sage
- 1 tablespoon mint
- 1 oak leaf
- 1 acorn

• Chamomile tea (enough to fill the bottle)
• Green candle

Procedure

Arrange the altar and cast the circle. When you are ready, charge the herbs to bring money into your life for as long as the bottle remains sealed. Next, charge the green candle to bring the power of growth and success to your spell. After this charging, light the green candle, settle yourself before the altar, and go into a meditation. After you are relaxed, begin a visualization of your intended goal for the bottle. See and feel yourself being happy, successful, and financially secure. After the visualization, begin filling the bottle. First, add your hair or nail clippings. Then add the herbs. Add the tea last. Tightly cork the bottle and then drip wax from the green candle on the cork (or lid) to seal it and bind your spell. Chant:

> *Security, freedom, and growth,*
> *In form of money, now come forth.*
> *Remove the worry, close the door—*
> *Bring comfort to me, fortune ensure!*

Place the bottle somewhere that you will be able to see it often but where it won't be disturbed by others (preferably in the kitchen or on the mantel). To invigorate its power, you may gently shake it from time to time during the waxing moon. It is done.

seven

Poppet Magic

A poppet is a cloth, clay, carved wood, straw, or wax figure used as a representation of a person or animal during magical work. Poppets are mainly used in magic designed to affect people rather than situations. The poppet is used in a process known today as sympathetic magic. Sympathetic magic works by creating a spiritual link by similar properties (such as making a poppet to look roughly like a person). The poppet is then loaded with items that once belonged to the person that still contain a portion of that person's energy, such as nail clippings, locks of hair, etc. Last, the poppet is consecrated and named to magically "be" that person. The poppet is then used in ritual to affect that person (or animal) in the desired way.

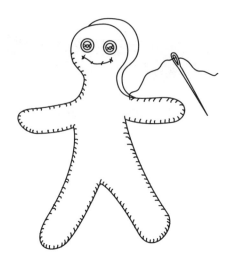

If the poppet is made of cloth, clay, or wax, then herbs and symbolic items are worked into it or used to fill it; if, however, the poppet is constructed of wood or straw, then herbs, symbols, and symbolic items may be attached to the outside of the doll. Here, you will only learn to make a cloth poppet. A cloth poppet is relatively easy to make, and a poppet that you make yourself will be infinitely more powerful than one that is store-bought.

Cloth Poppet

Items needed:

- Sewing needle
- Scissors
- Natural-fiber thread (in an appropriate color according to magical goal)
- Natural-fiber fabric (in an appropriate color)

• Herbs, personal items belonging to the
spell's target, and any other items to stuff
in the poppet

Procedure

Fold the fabric in half and cut out a "gingerbread man" human
shape about six inches to one foot in height. Now, thread the
needle and stitch the pieces together around the perimeter of
the human shape. Leave a small space open at the head or side
of the body (wide enough to get two fingers through), so that
you may turn the figure inside out (to hide the stitches). You
can then stuff it with the necessary ingredients and sew the
small opening closed. It may be decorated if desired.

After the poppet has been fully constructed, it is necessary to name it as the individual that you wish to affect
before using it in your spell.

Naming Ritual

The naming ritual is used to create a psychic link between
a poppet and the subject of a spell. Have the poppet stuffed
with the appropriate herbs and personal items from the subject of the spell. Place a censer (with appropriate incense)
and the knife in the north part of the altar, a bowl of salt in
the southeast, and a bowl of water in the southwest. Set the
cauldron in the center. Have a beeswax or appropriately colored candle in front of the cauldron.

Take a cleansing bath, arrange the altar, and cast the circle. During this rite, continually concentrate on the subject
of the spell. Take the poppet and pass it over the candle flame
and say, "You are charged with the power of will." Then, pass

the poppet over the censer and say, "You are charged with the power of thought." Next, place the poppet in the cauldron, sprinkle it with salt, and say, "You are charged with the power of being." Finally, sprinkle water over the poppet while saying, "You are charged with the power of feeling."

Next, summon energy and take the poppet in your weak hand and the knife in your strong hand. As you pour energy through the knife into the poppet, strongly visualize the person whom the poppet represents while chanting at least three times:

> *With flame of spirit and by sky, by land,*
> *and by sea, [name] you are now represented to me.*
> *All that you are is now a part of [he/she],*
> *[name], you are now represented to me.*

As you close the rite, say:

> *In the name of [chosen deity], so it shall be.*

Unnaming Ritual

The unnaming ritual is used in order to remove the identity attached to a poppet used in prior magic when a spell has been removed or reversed. Take the poppet and wash it with cold, blessed saltwater while saying the following at least three times:

> *I take away your name, strip your power, cut the tether,*
> *Your link to [name], broken,*
> *You are nameless, now and forever.*

After the poppet is washed and the name removed, take apart the doll and bury the bits in the ground so that the earth will absorb it and it will lose any remaining connection to the person for which it was named.

Bonding Spell

This spell is old and designed to bring together two people in marriage. Use this spell with caution and proper intent. A word of caution: Do not use this spell as a means of forcing another to do your bidding. Use it when you truly believe that two people love each other and want to get married, but something (nerves, outside influences, etc.) is holding them back. Cast the spell to remove their fear or obstacles and pave the way for the future that they desire. There is much potential for misuse of this spell, but I am including it here because it is traditional. In truth, any spell has the potential for misuse.

Items needed:

- 2 poppets (a poppet to represent each person)
- Personal items from each person
  (to stuff or attach to the poppets)
- Red cord
- Love incense (see page 208)
- Red candle (for the left)
- Pink candle (for the right)
- Red or pink cloth bag made of
  natural fiber (to hold the poppets)

Procedure

Take a cleansing bath, arrange the altar, and cast the circle. Create and name the poppets. Light the love incense, then the left candle, and finally the right candle. Go into a meditation. When you are ready, focus on the couple and a loving sense of the bond that they share. In your mind's eye see them embrace, see them at their wedding, and call out a heartfelt plea to your chosen deity, such as Hera, the Greek Goddess of marriage, asking that the couple be brought together in marriage if both of their true wills are to be together. Next, pick up both poppets, female in the left hand, male in the right (if applicable), and infuse your loving thoughts, emotion, and desire into the bodies of the poppets.

Now, join the poppets together in an embrace. Slowly wrap the pair with the red cord, binding them together. While you do this, visualize the couple being married and lovingly hugging each other. When you have finished binding the pair, tie a knot in the ends of the cord and place the poppets in the cloth bag. This ritual is best performed on the night before the full moon because the last step of this spell must take place on the full moon.

Finally, at midnight on the night of the full moon go to a dirt crossroads (previously selected) and bury the cloth bag containing the poppets in the center of the crossroads, asking that the couple will be married within the year if it is by the couple's free wills to be together. The year timeframe is traditional, but you can ask for a longer amount of time if desired. If you cannot find a dirt crossroads, you may take cornmeal or wheat flour and pour a plus sign on a patch of ground and bury the bundle next to it. After the bundle is buried, leave the crossroads without looking back. It is done.

Binding Spell

A binding spell is used to restrict the actions of another in order to prevent them from doing harm. It is powerful magic that definitely straddles the ethical boundary; it should only be used in cases of clear need and after all else fails. One of the dangers in using this spell frequently is becoming attached to the feeling of dominant power that goes along with the spell's successful results. The other danger is causing harm, whether through the thoughtless use of this spell on an innocent person or through improper, angry, vengeful use on a "deserving" person. Be wary of misuse.

Items needed:

- Poppet made to represent the person in question, stuffed with nettle, mullein, and elder flowers along with personal items from the one to be affected
- Black candle
- Binding incense (see page 205)
- Red, black, and gray ribbon or natural cord braided together

Procedure

The spell is best performed the day after the full moon or a Saturday during the waning moon for Saturn's influence. Take a cleansing bath, arrange the altar, and cast the circle. Make a cloth poppet. To stuff the poppet, gather together personal items or photographs of the one to be affected and the proper herbs. Name the poppet with the naming ritual.

Tie the ribbons or cords together in a single knot at the end. Hold the knot in your teeth and slowly braid together the ribbons while concentrating on the outcome of the binding. At the same time, gently rock back and forth with a "pulling" sense to draw the outcome to you. When the braiding is complete, tie a knot at the other end of the ribbons to complete your binding cord.

Now hold the poppet and imagine the person it represents bound in gray ropes, much like a mummy. Firmly tie the braided cord around the poppet, binding all parts that could possibly do harm. Next, charge it by saying:

No longer suffering by your hand,
Torment, strife, brute force be bound.
With this cord, I now entwine,
Peace and comfort shall be found,
In the name of [chosen deity], your power I bind!

This is followed by specific commands told to the poppet as if it were the actual person (it is a psychic link to them). These commands must be precise and "positively" phrased, meaning "I want" language rather than "I don't want" language. Some examples are, "I want you to avoid my presence" or "You must stay out of my sister's life." The wording must be in terms of what you want, spoken of in the present tense and definite, as opposed to, "I don't want to see you anymore" or "I don't want you to use drugs." The mind seems to respond more to "positive" language and phrasing. Remember to feel fully the relief of having the person finally bound.

Once you've given the command(s), place the poppet in a blessed spell box (see Chapter 10) or wrap it in black silk cloth and hide it away until you are ready to remove the spell. Burying the poppet may be done if you wish the binding to be permanent, but the spell would be much harder to undo once the poppet is buried. In a binding spell, burning the poppet is not recommended.

Unbinding Spell

It should be emphasized that it is harder to remove a binding spell (or any spell in general) than it is to cast one. This rite requires a lot of energy in order for it to break the original binding and may need to be repeated at regular intervals. The unbinding ritual can be used to help someone break free from an addiction or obsession, if you see the condition as a form of binding.

Items needed:
- Poppet
- Black candle (for the left)
- White candle (for the right)
- Unhexing oil (see page 216)
- Power incense (see page 212)
- Scissors or a knife

Procedure

If you were the one to bind the person in question, use the same poppet from the original binding spell in this ritual to free them. If not, or if you no longer have the doll, you must construct a new poppet, name it after the individual you wish to unbind, and wrap it in white cord to represent their condition. If you have to make a new poppet, it is recommended that it be constructed out of white wax, clay, or straw, as it does not have to be stuffed with anything and can have a personal item attached to the outside.

To begin the ritual, take a cleansing bath, arrange your altar, anoint the candles with the unhexing oil, cast the circle, and name the poppet with the naming ritual. After you have named the poppet, go into a meditation while holding the poppet. Imagine the poppet is bound in gray ropes, much like a mummy. Now see the ropes breaking and falling away from the poppet. Open your eyes and cut the poppet's cords while chanting:

> *These bonds are now broken—*
> *[Name], you are now free.*
> *Strength and free will are yours again,*
> *As I will, so it shall be!*

This chant is followed by specific commands told to the poppet as if it were the actual person (remember, the poppet is a psychic link to that person). These commands must be precise and "positively" phrased. Some examples are, "You desire healthy food" or "You are free of the one who tries to control you."

Once you have given the command(s), place the poppet in a prepared box and hide it away or give it to the person whom the poppet represents. Unbinding spells are best done during the waning moon.

Healing Spell

Healing spells can be tricky. When attempting to heal someone in pain, you need to know the correct diagnosis in order to properly treat the condition. It is important to know why a person is in pain to avoid treating only the pain; treating the pain alone masks the source of the problem and leaves it to fester. Before you even consider using magic to heal, your "patient" must go to a doctor and you should advise them to seek all available modern Western treatments. Healing spells can be used in conjunction with other medical treatments, energetically enhancing the effects of the conventional treatments as well as providing healing effects of their own. In using healing magic, it is best to make sure that your intent is to make the patient whole. For this reason, this spell is shown in a general way to avoid any magical errors. The energy is sent to make the patient whole, which should heal whatever ailments need healing.

As you advance, this spell should ideally be done with a poppet made from light-blue wax into which you have worked thyme, mint, sage, and some hair or nail clippings from the person needing to be healed. Because you will not be instructed in how to create wax poppets here, this spell will be described with a cloth poppet (simply stuff it with the herbs and personal items as previously instructed). If you do know how to create a wax poppet, they may be interchanged.

Items needed:
- Poppet (prepared, made from wax or cloth)
- Light-blue candle (for the left)
- White candle (for the right)
- Healing oil (see page 208)
- Healing incense (see page 207)
- Clear quartz crystal (small, add more if necessary)

Procedure

To begin the ritual, take a cleansing bath, arrange your altar, cast the circle, and name the poppet with the naming ritual. Anoint the candles with the healing oil. Go into a meditation and visualize the "patient" in a completely healed state. Raise healing energy by visualizing pure white light streaming into your body through your third eye and up into you from the earth. Pick up the poppet and infuse it with this energy by sending the light through your hands into the poppet. Place the poppet back on the altar and charge the crystal with healing energy in the same manner. Now, place the crystal on the poppet, over the area of the body most affected by the illness. If there are multiple areas of the body affected, then you will need as many crystals as necessary. After you place the crystal, sweep your hands over the poppet in a clockwise circular motion to remove any negative or unhealthy energy from the afflicted person. After you sweep away the negative energy, chant the following:

> *Wrapped in magic, healing power,*
> *Strengthen your body, every hour.*
> *[chosen deity], Goddess/God of earth and stars*
> *Wrap your arms around this one*
> *and heal him/her of all harms.*

As you chant, visualize that the patient is fully healed and strong. Wrap the poppet and crystal(s) in white cloth of a natural fiber and keep in a safe place until the healing has been successful.

Reversal of Fortune

This spell is worked when a wrongdoer seems to be getting away with a crime. This spell calls for nonspecific justice to come upon the person to correct the wrong that has been committed. There are two important keys to this spell. First, this spell must only be performed on someone who has committed a genuine wrong, otherwise it will turn back on the spell caster. Second, nonspecific justice is the only goal that must be kept in mind, and the feeling of relief must be kept in your heart throughout the casting. If these conditions are not met by the spell caster, this spell could act as a curse and cause damage to both the sender and target. With this spell you must trust that the deities will know how to properly handle the wrongdoer and that the best correction to their behavior will be found without your specification. This magic hurries the natural cosmic balancing (karma) that would already occur in the wrongdoer's life.

Items needed:

- Cloth poppet (named after the target and stuffed with nettle leaves and personal items belonging to the target)
- Cauldron
- Black candle
- Shovel (to dig a hole outside if you intend to bury the poppet)

Procedure

First, take a cleansing bath, cast a circle, and name the poppet with the naming ritual. With the poppet in your hands, in your own words ask the deities to ensure that justice is truly delivered to the wrongdoer and that the wrongdoer is stopped from committing further harm. Burn the poppet in the cauldron. If you cannot burn the poppet in the cauldron, cut a doorway in the circle, take the poppet outside, and bury the doll in the ground. Chant the following:

> *For what was done, justice is due,*
> *hastened and strengthened, three times three.*
> *What was sent out returns to you, as I will, so shall it be.*

If the poppet was burned, open the circle and end the rite, then bury the remains in the ground. If the poppet was only buried, return to the circle, thank the deities, and end the rite by thanking the deities and opening the circle. The wearing of a protective amulet is advisable until you are sure that the spell has taken effect.

Unhexing Spell

This spell will help you cleanse your body, mind, and spirit of negative energy. It will remove a curse if one has been cast upon you and can be cast upon another hexed individual.

Items needed:
- Beeswax or gray candle (for the left)
- Beeswax or white candle (for the right)
- White cloth poppet named after yourself (or the victim of the hex) and stuffed with barley and personal items
- Cauldron or heat-proof bowl (to be used as a censer)

• Unhexing oil (see page 216)

• Unhexing incense (see page 216)

Procedure

First, take a cleansing bath. Cast your circle with everything necessary for the rite inside. Make the cloth poppet and name it with the naming ritual. Dress the candles with unhexing oil. Go into a meditation. When you are relaxed, visualize the hexed person as perfectly happy, healthy, and surrounded by an aura of pure, white light. When you are ready, pick up the poppet and transfer this energy into the doll. Next, set the poppet on the altar and light the candles and the incense. Anoint the poppet on the head, chest, and genital regions with unhexing oil. See this oil as cleansing the hexed individual of any and all negativity. Pick up the doll once more and state the following with conviction:

> Loathsome cloud, heavy and bleak
> Loose your grip on one so dear.
> Darkness withdraw, [name] is released
> I call an end to negativity and fear!

After chanting, it is a good idea to add a blessing element so that the "energy vacuum" of cleansing is filled in with positive energy. You may state:

> You are now blessed and pure.
> New joy and purpose fills your life, blessed be.

The poppet should be wrapped in white cloth and kept safe.

eight

Cord and Knot Magic

In magical history, spinning and weaving to create knots, threads, and cords goes back countless centuries. To create one thing from another is seen as a magical act in and of itself. When a witch weaves together a cord—tying knots and chanting with sweetly scented smoke swirling in air illuminated only by candlelight—the witch is creating an object with a specific intention out of the randomness of the individual components, harnessing potential through a deliberate act of will. This action focuses the energy and leads to a powerful tool of manifestation. Cords and knots are used as elements in a number of spells found in this book, so it is a good idea to examine the use of cords as magical devices in their own right.

To be magically effective, any material used in cord magic should be of natural fibers. Synthetic fibers no longer carry their own life energy; whatever natural energies were in the raw materials used in their creation have been processed beyond recognition. The cords themselves should be in a symbolic color appropriate to your goal, as should any other items used. There is a basic procedure to the creation of each of these magical cords. I will give it as a template rather than be needlessly repetitive in describing the basics for each intention.

The basic process is to gather your ingredients, ritually bathe, cast your circle, meditate, and finally assemble and charge your cord. In the making of a cord, certain items are frequently stuck through the knots and braids in the cord in order to enhance its magical strength. These may either be added during the knotting and braiding process or added afterward just prior to the charging of the cord. I prefer to add them last because you otherwise risk breaking the items as you continue to braid the cord. These cords are made by first tying a single knot in three lengths of twine, string, yarn, or ribbon on one end, then braiding them together while you focus on the intent and rock slowly back and forth to "pull" the goal to you. Once the length has been braided, tie a second knot at the other end of the cord. This is followed by tying seven more knots in the cord, the same distance apart. Do this by tying one on the left side, then one on the right, gradually moving inward toward the center. Once completed, it is charged in the usual way (see Charging Ritual, page 75). I will give the correct incense and correspondences for each intention. It is best to use the "basic altar layout" when making these cords.

Cord Instructions

Love: Use white, pink, and red cord. To the knotted cord, add an apple twig, a rose bud, a lock of your own hair, a white feather, a small bell, a seashell, and a beloved piece of jewelry (earrings work well). In the charging ritual, use love incense and the appropriate love oil to anoint a red (left) and pink (right) candle and the cord itself.

Money: Use green, gold, and royal blue cord. To the knotted cord, add an oak twig, coins tied in a green cloth bag, chamomile flowers or a chamomile tea bag, a key, a lodestone wrapped in wire or placed in a gold bag, the amount of money that you need written on parchment (which is then rolled up and poked through the cord), and a drop of blood or saliva. In the charging ritual, use money incense and money oil to anoint a green (left) and gold (right) candle and the cord itself.

Power: Use yellow, red, and purple cord. To the knotted cord, add your own blood, a clear crystal, seven pine needles, an oak twig, a sprig of mint, a metal (preferably iron) spiral, and a crescent moon charm. In the charging ritual, use power incense and power oil to anoint a red (left) and purple (right) candle and the cord itself. Protection: Use blue, black, and red cord. To the knotted cord, add a sprig of mistletoe, an iron nail, a hazel twig, a rowan twig, a birch twig, an ash twig, and a small bag of salt. In the charging ritual, use protection incense and protection oil to anoint a black (left) and red (right) candle and the cord itself.

Spirituality: Use purple, indigo, and white cord. To the knotted cord, add a lock of hair, a moonstone, a willow twig, a small image or medallion of your personal deity, a white feather, a black feather, and a piece of driftwood or a seashell. In the charging ritual, use spirituality incense and spirituality oil to anoint an indigo (left) and purple (right) candle and the cord itself.

There are many more uses for magical cords. Some people create cords to capture the essence of each holiday or moon phase while others use cords to capture elemental energy. Cords are frequently used to alter weather patterns, and knotted cords can be used as something akin to prayer beads. Imagination is the only limitation to their use. Be creative, but remember to follow the basic outline for their creation and to always use items in harmony with your stated goal. Once you have a cord, there is much that can be done with it. You can hang it up on a wall by tying a loop in it or tying a bow; you can coil it up and place it in a charm bag to carry with you; or you can hide it somewhere it can send out its energy but remain undisturbed (like under the bed or in a drawer). The options are many.

nine

Verbal Magic

It is not always possible, necessary, or desired to conduct a full-fledged (or even a scaled-down) magical ritual. Luckily, there are simple spells that can be cast by simply focusing your energy and speaking them out loud. You first need to relax and move into a meditative state. Then, focus on your goal and the feeling you wish to have when your goal is reached. Speak your spell and mentally infuse the spell with your energy and intent. Blessings are the main focus of verbal spells, but they can also be used for protection, healing, minor banishing, "invisibility," growth, luck, and attraction.

Blessing for a Newborn Infant

Touch the infant on the forehead with blessed water and chant:

New little spirit, may your life be blessed;
May your words ring true and your mind be sharp;
May your heart know love and your body be strong;
May your path be gentle and your life be long.
Blessed be.

Blessing before Divination

This can be spoken before any form of divination to help channel the correct energy and protect you from not only the negative energies that may be present but also from any positive energy that might be present. Though not necessarily harmful, foreign energies might not be in harmony with your goal and could act as a hindrance (which is harmful to your work). For this blessing, chant:

I call upon the all-knowing Goddess to bless
my work with safety and success.
Please protect me from all positive and negative
energies and forces that would come and do me harm
and grant me knowledge of the past, present, future,
and the other worlds.
For the good of all and with harm to none, I dedicate
this work to you.

Blessing on a Task

Visualize yourself successfully completing a task before you while you chant the following:

Luck and skill light my way,
Pave my path with grace.
Blessed be myself this day,
As I complete [task], this task I face.

Blessing before a Voyage

When you are in or on a vehicle (car, boat, whatever), visualize a protective bubble around yourself and the entire vehicle and chant the following to yourself:

Earth beneath please guide my steps;
Stars above please light my way;
Bless and protect me on my journey,
Keep [me/us] safe through night and day.

House Blessing

Bring a special gift to the house such as a new broom (whether practical or decorative) or a "kitchen witch"-style poppet. Charge this gift with protective qualities beforehand, and once you place this gift in its new home, you are ready to begin the blessing. To work a house blessing, you attempt to fill each room in the house with warm, loving, welcoming energy to fill the energetic void left in the house from a lack of occupants. Go from room to room in a clockwise direction, beginning and ending at the front door. Say the following chant with outstretched arms, projecting the loving energy from your hands:

Living space, you are pure and free;
Peaceful and happy, a nurturing den;
Filled with warmth, blessed be,
A place of joy, a home again.

Growth Spell

This spell can be said over plants in your garden. Cup your hands over the plant and focus on the plant in a sturdy, full bloom state as you chant:

> *From seed to shoot to bud,*
> *Your journey paved with magic power.*
> *Grow strong and healthy, stretch high above,*
> *Root and stem and leaf and flower.*

Neutralizing Negativity

If there is a difficult person in your life causing negativity and conflict, this spell can be used to neutralize their influence without causing them harm. Visualize the person in your mind (it helps to have a photo of the person in front of you) and see them wrapped in white cords as if they are being bound. See these cords shift in color to gray; gradually, the person is nothing more than a gray shadow. While visualizing, chant:

> *The lines blur, your power falls;*
> *Force of conflict, turn to gray;*
> *With harm to none, for good of all;*
> *Your influence negated and swept away.*

Protection

If you feel in need of protection, visualize yourself surrounded by a bubble of white light that condenses and "solidifies" into a shining, mirrored orb that repels any and all negativity and danger. As you visualize, chant the following:

Shield of power, protect me from harm,
From threat of danger, negativity, and storm;
Glowing power, mirrored might,
Keep me safe with your magic light.

Invisibility

This spell is useful when you wish to be left alone. Now, I must emphasize that this spell will not make you physically invisible—sorry! Rather, it will "take you off the radar" by blurring the energy you send out so you are much less noticeable, and in many instances, people will not see or notice you until you actually touch them. To start off, close your eyes and visualize yourself encased in a glowing bubble of silvery-white light. When you have this image in your mind, begin to see the bubble of light blur and fade. As the light fades, the image of yourself should also fade until you are completely invisible in your mind's eye. As you are doing this, chant the following:

Surrounded by the magic light,
Cloaked within its mystic blur,
Invisibility wrought through your might,
Until I wish my form returned.

When you wish to no longer be "invisible," you must visualize the invisible bubble gradually becoming more and more visible and definite. Once the bubble is clearly seen, visualize the energy dispersing, leaving a clear, solid image of you. Then open your eyes.

Banishing

This spell can be used to send away a bothersome person, entity, or animal without causing harm. You must remain neutral in your intention, wishing only to send them out of your life. While casting this spell, in your mind's eye, see the target of the spell cupped in the two hands of the Goddess. As you speak the words, see her drawing the target of the spell away from you until you can no longer see them anymore.

> *Goddess rid me of this conflict,*
> *Take away my strife;*
> *Rid me of this block,*
> *Remove it from my life;*
> *Without harm and blessed be,*
> *May we both be now set free.*

Healing

This type of healing would only be used for the relief of minor aches and pains or to speed the healing of cuts and scrapes. For larger ailments, full-scale ritual would need to be performed (or, of course, a trip to the doctor). For a quick burst of healing energy, go into your meditative state and hold your projective hand over the area of the body to be healed and send energy out from your hand into the injury. While doing so, chant:

> *Harmony, strength, and balance,*
> *The body heals and is restored;*
> *Soothe and relax, heal and mend—*
> *Painful suffering at an end.*

To Bring Luck

Fill your mind with a pleasant inner calm, using one of the meditations given in Part 1 if desired. Visualize things going your way and feel the peace and happiness that will bring you. When you are ready, chant:

My path before me, with hope I tread;
Good fortune shall to me be led;
With open heart to light my way,
Good luck to me throughout my day.

Attraction

If you wish to surround yourself with an aura of enchantment that will attract others to you, visualize yourself surrounded by a pink bubble of light and chant the following three times:

Sparkle, glow, and glamoury,
Does here and now envelop me.
Drawn like a magnet, moths to a flame,
Attraction my goal, attraction my aim!

Magical Safekeeping

We've all heard tales of treasure chests, magic trunks, powerful rings, magical lockets, and of secret mysteries hidden away. We've heard of these mysteries bundled into the hollow of a fabled faery tree under the cover of darkness with the moon above as the only witness. As fanciful as it sounds, things like this do happen every day all over the world. These tools are a means of securing our magic, keeping it strong and focused on making our wishes come true.

With some spells, such as those that require poppets or paper, it is advised that that you store the item in a safe place. So where is this safe place? The answer is simple: in a spell box. A spell box is a box that has been cleansed and consecrated for use in holding magical items for the duration of a spell (or beyond). Any type of box can be used, but a wooden box is traditional. You can either make your own spell box or you can buy a small treasure-chest box and consecrate it. You could also use an old keepsake box, a glass or ceramic bowl, or a large jar as long as it has a lid. A few years ago, my sister hollowed out and carved a gourd for me and created an image of a wolf and a pentagram on its surface. This gourd makes a fantastic protective-oriented spell box. Almost anything can be used. After you choose or create a box, the box must be cleansed and consecrated.

Cleansing a Spell Box

Cleansing the spell box in the following method is recommended if the box is old or has been used for other purposes before. To cleanse the spell box, close your eyes while holding the box and visualize white light pouring down on you from above. Imagine the light streaming from your hands into the box, cleansing it of any negativity. If you wish, you could hold the box in the smoke of purification incense (see page 214) for a few moments, making sure that all parts of the box are touched by the smoke.

Next, the box must be charged with the same type of energy as the item that will be stored. For example, if you intend to store a poppet used in a healing rite, then you should fill the spell box with healing energy, loading it as if it were a talisman. This provides a wonderful boost to your original spell and prevents the poppet's energies from being scattered. After you no longer need to store the poppet in that box, just cleanse and consecrate the spell box for a new use.

Never reuse a spell box without cleansing and conse-crating it again. The box will still contain residual energy from the previous spell; this residue will cloud and confuse the new spell, thus altering or reducing your results. Aside from being a magical safe place and power booster, a spell box is a practical storage item if you are worried that your magical items will be seen or handled by others. If that is the case, I suggest obtaining the most inconspicuous, plain, unremarkable box you can find; the less noticeable the bet-ter. You can use a large trunk as a spell box to store your ritual items and tools to keep them safe, properly energized, and out of the hands of others. In this instance, the box or trunk should be charged with general magical energy (white light from the universe). This will keep the tools safe without blending or scattering their individual energies.

Spell boxes can be used as magical devices in their own right. To do this, first you must decide on a goal and obtain ingredients in harmony with that goal, such as herbs, photos, fabrics, etc. Next, design a decorative theme for the spell box that illustrates your goal. The process is kind of like making a dollhouse. Decorate your spell box in such a way that just by looking at it, you know what you are working toward. It is your vision made manifest. For example, if I was making a spell box for a new home, a good idea would be to obtain a photo of the type of home I was looking for (or a specific home as long as it is currently for rent or sale) and glue it inside the box. I would add herbs for prosperity, a lock of my hair to lend my own personal energy, and maybe even some doll furniture in a style that appeals to me. Let your imagi-nation run with possibility. Decorate your box how you see fit; as long as its decoration is in harmony with your magical goal, your results should be splendidly successful. After the decorating is complete, charge the box with magical energy to be a talisman toward your goal.

Keep the spell box in a safe place where you can see it often. Spell boxes are great magical storage devices and a wonderful method of gathering multiple ingredients into one spell, as in the "new home" example above. Another more portable method takes the form of a locket or "poison ring." A locket, of course, is a small case with a hinged lid that may contain a photo or other small item and is usually worn as a pendant. A poison ring is similar, as it too is a small container with a hinged lid that is worn as a ring. Both of these items may be transformed into tools of magic. By placing an herb, photo, jewel, or lock of hair into a locket or ring and magically charging it, you recreate it as a talisman.

This form of talisman is excellent for keeping magical energy around you without drawing too much attention to yourself. A giant flannel bag worn around your neck while strolling through the grocery store would be a bit awkward; magical jewelry is a much more practical alternative. Another benefit is that since you can only store a tiny amount in a locket, the cost of herbs or other ingredients is minimized. You can charge them with the general charging ritual (see Charging Ritual on page 75).

Finally, we come to a beautiful method of working magic with the aid of trees. Trees are beautiful, wise, long-lived beings that are grounded into the earth, reach to the sky, and drink in the rain. They are connected to all three realms of land, sea, and sky and are natural conduits for reaching from realm to realm and through the different planes of existence. Each tree (like all living things) is made of both its physical self and its spirit (the tree faery). If a tree contains an uninhabited hollow (a natural hollow—don't drill a hole in a tree for this), you can store a bundle or charm bag there and ask the tree spirit to help you manifest your goal. You can write your wish on a piece of paper and hide it in the hollow of the tree and ask for the tree's assistance. If you seek the aid of a tree, or any living thing for that matter, always leave a token of gratitude in addition to what you leave there as your magical petition. For trees, leave water, compost, or fertilizer.

A final note regarding trees: If you feel uneasy, nervous, or rejected around a particular tree, don't ask for its help. This is the way the spirit of the tree is letting you know it doesn't want to participate for whatever reason. An unhappy tree spirit would only hurt your chances of achieving your goal. If the spirit is not inclined to you, don't worry—it will let you know.

eleven

Nature Magic:
Land, Sea, Sky, and
Sacred Fire Spells

I have chosen to include some spells specifically designed to call on the power of the three realms found in Irish witch-craft—land, sea, and sky—as well as sacred fire. Sacred fire is above and apart from the other three. In modern Wicca, these spells would be used to invoke the elements of earth, water, air, and fire. As magic is done through channeling and directing natural energies, a rapport with nature will enhance and empower your magical work. For this reason, it is important to make a conscious effort to attune yourself to the natural world and recognize the beauty and life forces contained therein before working with the elemental realms.

I will give the outlines of four spells that have stood the test of time that you can modify to fit your specific goals. There are certain goals and attributes that resonate with each element and realm individually. Land spells are good for grounding, wealth, protection, and the home. Sea spells are good for love, psychic ability, emotional issues, and healing. Sky spells are good for the mind, persuasion, communication, and cleansings. Fire spells are good for focusing the power of will, making them helpful for any goal but specifically invocation, force, war, creation, destruction, and power.

Land Spell

Items needed:
- 3 black or brown cords
- Piece of paper with your goal written on it
- 3 or 7 herbs that align with your goal
- Small paper or natural-fiber cloth bag

Procedure
Define your intent and make sure that it corresponds to the qualities of the land. Next, gather together the cords, piece of paper with your goal, herbs, and the small bag. You may add any other items you feel also represent what you wish to achieve as long as they are biodegradable. Place the paper and the herbs into the bag and set the bag in front of you. Sit in a comfortable position or in a rocking chair and tie the three cords together on one end. Go into a meditation. When you are relaxed, focus on your goal. While keeping the goal in mind, hold the knot in the cords between your teeth and slowly braid the cords together. As you do this,

rock gently back and forth and create a kind of "tugging" sense to help draw the goal to you.

As you braid the cord, you must tie a knot representing your wish at least two more times (at least once in the middle and one more at the other end), though a total of nine knots is the ideal. After you have braided the cord, use it to tie up the bag. Then, cup the bag in your hands, summon energy, and breathe this energy into the bag while chanting a short rhyme that you have composed to achieve your goal. Finally, bury the bundle outside, preferably beneath an herb or tree that is in harmony with your goal, asking that they help your wish to manifest. It is done.

Sea Spell

Items needed:
- Bottle
- Odd number of herbs that align to your goal
- Piece of paper with your goal
  written on it; burned to ash
- Cauldron
- 2 cups of water

Procedure
With this spell, you will be making a potion that is then dispersed into the water as a gift to that realm and as a beacon of your intent. First, heat about two cups of spring water in your cauldron. When it begins to steam, toss in the herbs. While the herbs are brewing, write your goal on a piece of paper and focus all your thoughts, emotions, and energy into the paper. Next, burn the paper (safely) and sprinkle

the ashes into the brew. While the brew is cooling, go into a meditation. When you are relaxed, cup your hands over the cauldron and "sweep away" any inappropriate or foreign energy from the brew, leaving only the energy best suited to achieve your goal. Once the brew is completely cooled, bottle it and charge it as tool of your magical intent. Finally, go to a natural body of water. While calling upon the creatures and spirits of the waters to help you, pour the brew into the water and ask that your goal be reached. It is done.

Sky Spell

Items needed:
- Pestle and mortar
- 3 herbs that align with your goal
- Piece of paper with your goal written on it

Procedure

This spell requires a windy day. First, burn the piece of paper with your goal until it is ash (be sure to do this out of the wind). Next, using a pestle and mortar, grind the herbs and blend them with the ashes from the paper. Empower this mixture with your magical need and take this powder to an outdoor location, preferably a hill or mountain. Cup the powder in your hands and ask the spirits of the air and the gods of the sky to make your goal manifest. Then, scatter the herbs to the winds by sprinkling them in a clockwise circle around you. It is done.

Sacred Fire Spell

Items needed:

- Small piece of wood (about the size of your open hand)
- Ink or paint in a color appropriate to your goal
- Paintbrush or dip pen (depending)
- 3 herbs that align with your goal

Procedure

This formula is the basis of many spells. First, empower the wood and herbs with your intent and place the herbs in the unlit hearth or outdoor fire pit. Next, on the piece of wood, write or paint either your specific goal or a symbol that you feel properly represents your goal. Then, compose a rhyming chant that pertains to your goal and go to the fireplace. Light a fire with the herbs placed on the firewood. Stand before the fire, holding the small piece of wood you collected; call on your personal deity and ask them to help you in reaching your goal. As you do this, once again pour your energy and intent in to the wood piece. When you are ready, place the piece of wood into the fire while chanting your rhyme and visualizing your goal. When the fire burns out, it is done.

Each of the previous spells are relatively easy to perform and are useful for a wide variety of magical needs. (For ideas on which herbs are appropriate to use for each spell, see Appendix Two on page 231.) There are a number of good books out there on herbal magic and correspondence that may be consulted when designing and modifying spells.

Part III

Ingredients and Recipes

This section covers everything you will need to know in order to create the oils and incenses used in the spells and rituals throughout this book. It will also help you along the path of general herb magic, with a short reference guide to the herbs and their most common magical uses.

twelve

A Guide to the
Herbs of Magic

The following list is not complete, but it does contain all of the herbs used in the recipes in this book. It is also meant to be a guide to ingredients for creating your own recipes and in case you need to substitute any ingredients in the formulas in this book. If substitution is necessary, simply look at the list to find an herb with similar properties, magical uses, and correspondences to use in place of the original herb.

The herb list is organized alphabetically by common name, Latin name, gender (the polarity of the herb), planet associated with the herb, and finally, the herb's element. Individual herbs carry unique patterns of energy based on their genus and makeup. Herbs that are more "active" and "aggressive" are considered "male"; herbs that are more "subtle" and "gentle" in their mechanisms of action are considered "female." Herbs are tied to individual planets based on their energy patterns. Herbs of Venus, for example, all share a basic loving, delicate energy and can be used for similar goals.

Herbs

Angelica—*Angelica archangelica;* masculine; Sun; fire.
Magical uses: Angelica is used in magic related to exorcism, protection, and visions.

Apple blossom—*Pyrus spp.;* feminine; Venus; water. **Magical uses:** Apple blossoms smell wonderful and have been used in love and healing mixtures for centuries. Dried apple peels can be used if you have no access to a flowering apple tree.

Betony—*Stachys betonica;* masculine; Jupiter; fire. **Magical uses:** Betony is used for protection (especially at the summer solstice), purification, and to find love.

Bindweed—*Convovulus arvensis;* masculine; Saturn; water. **Magical uses:** Binding destructive habits, people, or forces.

Blackberry—*Rubus villosus;* feminine; Venus; water. **Magical uses:** The branches and fruits of blackberry are both used for protection.

Blackthorn—*Prunus spinosa;* masculine; Mars; fire. **Magical uses:** Used for exorcism and protection; the thorns are used as needles to stick in poppets, or added to witch bottles.

Caraway—*Carum carvi;* masculine; Mercury; air. **Magical uses:** This is used in spells and recipes for protection and to induce lust.

Catnip—*Nepeta cateria;* feminine; Venus; water. **Magical uses:** Catnip is used in love spells and to create a closer relationship between you and your cat (if you have one).

Chamomile—*Anthemis nobilis;* masculine; Sun; water. **Magical uses:** Chamomile is a strong money herb; it is used to bring love, purification, and in sleep mixtures.

Cinquefoil—*Potentilla canadensis;* masculine; Jupiter; fire. **Magical uses:** This is an all-purpose herb that can be used for nearly any desire, such as love, luck, money, health, and/or wisdom. It is also known as "five-finger grass" and it is said to protect against the evil that five fingers can do.

Clover—*Trifolium spp.;* masculine; Mercury; air. **Magical uses:** This herb is used for protection, money, love, and exorcism.

Comfrey—*Symphytum officinale;* feminine; Saturn; water. **Magical uses:** Comfrey can be used to bring money and for safety during travel. It has a visionary element to it.

Dandelion—*Taraxacum officinale;* masculine; Jupiter; air. **Magical uses:** This plant can be used to bring good luck, improve psychic ability, and call spirits.

Elder flowers—*Sambucus nigra;* feminine; Venus; water.
Magical uses: The branches, leaves, and flowers of the
elder tree are used in spells to expel everything from
illness to evil spirits. It is used to bring protection
and to connect with the Mother Goddess or bring her
energy into your life.

Eyebright—*Euphrasia officinalis;* masculine; Sun; air. **Magical uses:** Eyebright is used in spells to improve memory, reveal truth, and to induce clairvoyance.

Fumitory—*Fumaria officinalis;* feminine; Saturn; earth.
Magical uses: This is used in magic related to exorcism.

Hazel—*Carylus spp.;* masculine; Sun; air. **Magical uses:**
Hazel is known as the tree of wisdom; both the wood
and nuts are used to bring insight and knowledge into
your life. Hazel is used to bring protection and luck.

Heather—*Erica spp.;* feminine; Venus; water. **Magical uses:**
Heather is burned to cause ghosts to appear. It is used
to preserve chastity and to bring rain.

Holly—*Ilex aquifolium;* masculine; Mars; fire. **Magical
uses:** Holly has its strongest influence from the summer solstice to the winter solstice. Holly is used to
bring protection and luck into your life. It is one of the
classic herbs of the winter solstice and can be used to
fill the home with vitality during this cold time of year.

Juniper—*Juniperus communis;* masculine; Sun; fire. **Magical uses:** Both the berries and leaves of the juniper
bush are burned to bring protection or used in exorcisms. The berries can also be used for love.

Loosestrife—*Lythrum salicaria;* feminine; Moon; earth.
Magical uses: Loosetrife is used to bring protection,
peace, and the influence of the moon.

Marjoram—*Origanum vulgare;* masculine; Mercury; air.
Magical uses: Marjoram is an all-purpose herb and can
be used for protection, love, health, and money.

Meadow sage—*Salvia pratensis.* **Magical uses:** Any type of
sage, including the much more common *Salvia officinalis*, can be used for protection, healing, money, and
as an aid in spiritual cleansing.

Mint—*Menthe spp.;* masculine; Mercury; air. **Magical uses:**
Any form of mint can be used for healing, money
magic, and protection.

Mistletoe (American)—*Phoradendron leucarpum;* masculine; Mercury; air. **Magical uses:** Mistletoe can be used
for protection, luck, and love. It is poisonous.

Mistletoe (European)—*Viscum album;* masculine; Mercury; air. **Magical uses:** Revered by druids, European
mistletoe used to only be cut with a golden sickle and
has the same uses as its American counterpart.

Moonwort—*Botrychium spp.;* feminine; Moon; water.
Magical uses: Moonwort is used to bring in the influences of the Moon. It can be used to bring love or to
increase money by placing it among pieces of silver,
the moon's metal.

Mugwort—*Artemesia vulgaris;* feminine; Venus; earth.
Magical uses: Mugwort helps to open your psychic
perceptions; it can be used as a psychic enhancer via
incense, herbal pillows, oils, and more.

Mullein—*Verbascum thapsus;* feminine; Saturn; fire. **Magical uses:** Mullein is used for protection and exorcism
and to call on the influence of Saturn for stability.

Nettle—*Urtica dioica;* masculine; Mars; fire. **Magical uses:**
This is used in exorcism, protection, and hex breaking.
Use of nettle to remove a hex will send it back to its
sender.

Oak acorn—*Quercus alba;* masculine; Sun; fire. **Magical
uses:** The oak is considered to be a sacred tree and has
many magical uses. The wood, leaves, and acorns of
the oak can be used for fertility, health, luck, protection, and money.

Oak moss—*Evernia prunastri;* masculine; Jupiter; earth.
Magical uses: This is used in magic related to protection and money.

Parsley—*Petroselinum crispum;* masculine; Mercury; air.
Magical uses: Parsley can be used to bring lust, purification, and protection; it should not be cut by someone in love.

Pennyroyal—*Mentha pulegium;* masculine; Mars; fire.
Magical uses: Pennyroyal is used to bring strength
and protection.

Pine—*Pinus spp.;* masculine; Mars; air. **Magical uses:** Pine
is used for money, protection, and purification; it can

be used to bring life energy into the home through the cold winter months because it is an evergreen.

Raspberry—*Rubus strigosus;* feminine; Venus; water. **Magical uses:** The thorny (bramble) branches of the raspberry bush are used for protection; the berries are used to bring or enhance love.

Rose and rose hips—*Rosa spp.;* feminine; Venus; water. **Magical uses:** Roses of all sorts are used to bring love, for protection, and to enhance psychic ability through dreams.

Rowan—*Sorbus acuparia;* masculine; Sun; fire. **Magical uses:** Rowan is used to bring protection (particularly in the spring) and to enhance psychic ability.

Saint John's wort—*Hypericum perforatum;* masculine; Sun; fire. **Magical uses:** This herb brings protection and can be used in exorcism and banishing.

Seaweed (kelp)—*Fucus vesiculosus;* feminine; Moon; water. **Magical uses:** This attracts sea spirits and gives protection to those traveling on the ocean.

Strawberry—*Fragaria vesca;* feminine; Venus; water. **Magical uses:** Both the leaves and berries are used to enhance love and bring good luck. Use sparingly.

Thyme—*Thymus vulgaris;* feminine; Venus; water. **Magical uses:** A wonderful herb that attracts bees and faeries, thyme has a wide range of uses: health, psychic ability, love, and purification.

Valerian—*Valeriana officinalis;* feminine; Venus; water. **Magical uses:** This is used for purification and to induce sleep. Use very little—this herb has a foul odor.

Vervain—*Verbena officinalis;* feminine; Venus; earth. **Magical uses:** Vervain is used for protection, purification, and love.

Willow—*Salix spp.;* feminine; Moon; water. **Magical uses:** All forms of willow are used to call on the influences of the moon. Willow can be used for love magic.

Woodruff—*Asperula odorata;* masculine; Mars; fire. **Magical uses:** This is used in magic related to money, protection, and success.

Yarrow—*Achillea millefollium;* feminine; Venus; water. **Magical uses:** Yarrow can be used to enhance psychic ability, help in exorcisms, and keep a couple together happily for seven years.

thirteen

Potion Class: Creating Herbal Brews, Raw Incense, Magical Oils, and Salves

Brewing

For centuries, brewing magical potions has been associated with witches. Far from being an unfair stereotype, we do occasionally light a fire (usually on a kitchen stove), pour fresh water into our cauldrons (or an enamel pot), and as the water warms and steam rises, drifting through the air, we throw magically charged herbs into the water and let the infusion mingle the essences of the herbs into one powerful concoction! Cackling is optional, of course.

The actual process of brewing a potion is not really that difficult as long as you follow the steps and have all the necessary tools and ingredients. As a general rule, you would add a total of one ounce (two tablespoons) of herbal mixture per cup of water unless otherwise indicated in the recipe. Prior to adding the herbs for the brew, they should be ground, mixed, and empowered with your magical goal for the finished product. The water is heated in the chosen vessel (a cauldron or cooking pot dedicated to brew making) until it nears the boiling point and begins to steam; then herbs are added and the pot is covered with a lid, removed from the high heat, and left to steep for ten to thirteen minutes. After the brew has steeped, it is usually strained and bottled for use. This is the basic brewing process and will be modified in some instances. Some brews, particularly those with roots and barks as ingredients, require that you boil the water and herbs covered in order to properly extract the essence. In other cases, there will not be an opportunity to strain the brew, such as when you're brewing outdoors in a balefire; in that case, you will just have to carefully ladle out the brew into cups without straining. There are several brew recipes included in this book and any modifications that can be made are noted in the recipe. Brews should be made and immediately used. Their power diminishes greatly if they are left out or refrigerated.

Note: None of the recipes are intended to treat or cure any illness or condition. I have used the brews successfully to relieve my own symptoms over the years, but am not suggesting them as a replacement to traditional medical care.

Making Incense

Making incense is another relatively easy process. Grind the chosen recipe of herbs in a pestle and mortar, combine them in a bowl, and add any required liquid ingredients. Then all you have to do is empower the incense with your intent and bottle it for future use. To use the incense, simply light a quick-light charcoal (the kind designed for incense rather than for barbeque), place it in a censer, and sprinkle a bit of incense on the glowing charcoal. Add more incense as needed.

Making Oil

In magic, a variety of herbal and flower oils can be used. A few types are pure essential oils taken directly from the plant, oil blends designed to mimic the scent of a specific herb or flower, or extracted scent oils made by soaking or heating plant substances in a base oil until the plant essences are extracted. This last type of oil is what I prefer to use for a few reasons. Making scented oil is much cheaper than purchasing essential oils, and essential oils have to be diluted with a base oil; in addition, I find homemade scented oils to be more magical in their function than their purchased counterparts because scented oils require a bit more personal effort to create.

Making scented oils is pretty easy. You will need a pot, bottle, spoon, base oil, herbal ingredients, and a sieve to strain the finished oil. A base or carrier oil is relatively unscented oil that is used as the main ingredient in an oil recipe to extract and carry the scents and energies of the other ingredients. Frequently, vegetable (soy) oil is used as a carrier oil as are olive and jojoba oils, the latter being more of a liquefied wax than an actual oil. I prefer soy oil in most of my work, except for where olive oil is specifically called for in a recipe.

The basic formula for oils is four tablespoons of herbs to a half cup of base oil (vegetable or soy oil, olive oil, jojoba oil, sunflower oil, or grape seed oil are a few). You then pour the oil into a pot dedicated to this purpose (don't use the pot for food), mix in the herbs, and heat over very low heat, stirring constantly until the scent of the oil fills the air. Now, remove from heat, put the lid on the pot, and let the oil cool for half an hour. Once the oil has cooled, strain, bottle, and empower the oil with your intent. If the scent is not strong enough, you can reuse the same oil, adding fresh herbs and repeating the simmering process until the scent is strong enough. After the oil is complete, label the bottle and refrigerate.

Making Salves

The process of making herbal salves or ointments is not that complicated. It is essentially the same process as making scented magical oils except you use lard or vegetable shortening as your base instead of using liquid oil. First, grind and mix the chosen herbs. Next, slowly melt the shortening over LOW heat and stir in the herbs. Keep stirring until the scent of the herbs fills the air. When you can smell the herbs, remove the pot from the stove, let it cool slightly, and pour the liquid (carefully!) through a metal sieve and into a heatproof container. Allow the ointment to cool, and refrigerate when not in use. Ointments have minimal shelf life (about 3 days) and should only be made in small amounts when needed.

fourteen

Recipes

The recipes included here are the recipes called for in the spells of this book, plus a few extra brew recipes for general purposes.

Binding Incense
- 1 tablespoon mullein
- 1 tablespoon bindweed
- 1 tablespoon sage
- 1 tablespoon nettle
- 2 drops binding oil

Grind together all of the herbs, then moisten with the two drops of oil. Spread out on a plate or paper towel to dry for a few hours. Then, empower with your intent and place in a jar.

Binding Oil

- 1 tablespoon nettle
- 2 teaspoons mullein
- 1 teaspoon sage
- ¼ cup vegetable oil

Pour the oil into a small pot. Grind together the herbs and swirl them into the oil. Empower the mixture with your intent. Heat the oil on low, swirling the pot gently to mix in the herbs. After a minute or so when the oil has warmed enough to smell the herbs (not bubbling), remove from heat and let cool. Strain the cooled oil into a jar.

Familiar Incense

- 1 tablespoon catnip
- 1 tablespoon clover
- 1 tablespoon red rose petals

Grind the herbs together, empower them with your intent, and pour into a jar.

Familiar Oil

- 1 tablespoon cinquefoil
- 1 tablespoon dandelion
- ¼ teaspoon valerian
- ¼ cup oil

Grind and empower the herbs and then place them in a small pot with the oil. Swirl the oil over low heat until you can smell the mixture in the air. Let the oil cool and then strain into a jar.

Go-away Incense

- 1 tablespoon Saint John's wort
- 1 tablespoon betony
- 1 tablespoon heather

Grind the herbs together, empower them with your intent, and pour into a jar that you find unattractive.

Go-away Oil

- 2 teaspoons Saint John's wort
- 1 teaspoon elder flowers
- 1 tablespoon heather
- ¼ cup vegetable oil

Grind and empower the herbs and then place them in a small pot with the oil. Swirl the oil over low heat until you can smell the mixture in the air. Let the oil cool and then strain into a jar that you find unattractive.

Healing Incense

- 1 tablespoon juniper
- 1 tablespoon mint
- 1 tablespoon thyme

Grind the herbs together, empower them with your intent, and pour into a jar.

Healing Oil

- 2 teaspoon willow leaves
- 1 tablespoon oak leaves
- 1 teaspoon mint
- ¼ cup vegetable oil

Grind and empower the herbs and then place them in a small pot with the oil. Swirl the oil over low heat until you can smell the mixture in the air. Let the oil cool and then strain into a jar.

Love Incense

- 1 tablespoon red rose
- 2 teaspoons yarrow
- 1 tablespoon marjoram
- 1 teaspoon juniper
- 1 drop of apple juice
- 1 drop of red rose oil

Grind the herbs together, empower them with your intent, and moisten with the drop of apple juice and drop of oil. Spread out on a paper towel to dry; place in a pretty jar.

Love Oil (women)

- 1 tablespoon rose
- 2 teaspoons catnip
- 1 teaspoon ground strawberry leaves
- ¼ cup vegetable oil

Grind and empower the herbs and place them in a small pot with the oil. Swirl the oil over low heat until you can smell the mixture in the air. Let the oil cool and then strain into a jar. This oil needs to be made by and for heterosexual women only.

Love Oil (men)
- 1 tablespoon marjoram
- 2 teaspoons crushed juniper
- 1 teaspoon vervain
- ¼ cup vegetable oil

Grind and empower the herbs and place them in a small pot with the oil. Swirl the oil over low heat until you can smell the mixture in the air. Let the oil cool and then strain into a jar. This oil needs to be made by and for heterosexual men only.

Love Oil (gay men)
- 1 teaspoon marjoram
- 2 teaspoons juniper
- 1 tablespoon red rose
- ¼ cup vegetable oil

Grind and empower the herbs and place them in a small pot with the oil. Swirl the oil over low heat until you can smell the mixture in the air. Let the oil cool and then strain into a jar. This oil should be made by and for gay men only.

Love Oil (lesbians)
- 2 teaspoons catnip
- 1 teaspoon strawberry (mashed berry or leaves)
- 1 tablespoon vervain
- ¼ cup vegetable oil

Grind and empower the herbs and place them in a small pot with the oil. Swirl the oil over low heat until you can smell the mixture in the air. Let the oil cool and then strain into a jar. This oil needs to be made by and for lesbians only.

Luck Incense

- 3 dried holly leaves, crushed
- 1 tablespoon ground oak leaves
- 1 tablespoon strawberry leaves
- 1 small mashed strawberry

Grind the herbs together, mix them with the mashed strawberry, empower them with your intent, and spread the mixture on a paper towel to dry. When dry, bottle the incense for future use.

Luck Oil

- 1 teaspoon crushed holly berries
- 1 crushed acorn
- 1 tablespoon strawberry leaves
- ¼ cup vegetable oil

Grind and empower the herbs and then place them in a small pot with the oil. Swirl the oil over low heat until you can smell the mixture in the air. Let the oil cool and then strain into a jar.

Money Incense

- 1 tablespoon sage
- 1 tablespoon cinquefoil
- 1 tablespoon oak moss

Grind the herbs together, empower them with your intent, and place in a jar.

Money Oil

- 1 tablespoon oak leaves
- 1 tablespoon cinquefoil
- 1 tablespoon chamomile
- 1 teaspoon mint
- ½ cup vegetable oil

Grind and empower the herbs and then place them in a small pot with the oil. Swirl the oil over low heat until you can smell the mixture in the air. Let the oil cool and then strain into a jar.

Peace Incense

- 1 tablespoon apple blossom
- 1 tablespoon vervain
- 1 tablespoon loosestrife
- ¼ teaspoon olive oil

Grind the herbs and mix them with the oil. Empower the mixture with your intent and spread on a paper towel to dry. When the incense is dry, bottle it in a clear or white jar.

Peace Oil

- 1 tablespoon apple blossom
- 2 teaspoons vervain
- 1 teaspoon loosestrife
- ¼ cup vegetable or olive oil

Grind and empower the herbs and then place them in a small pot with the oil. Swirl the oil over low heat until you can smell the mixture in the air. Let the oil cool and then strain into a clear or white jar.

Power Incense

- 1 tablespoon pine needles
- 1 tablespoon oak leaves
- 1 tablespoon rowan leaves

Grind herbs, empower them with your intent, and place in a jar.

Power Oil

- 1 tablespoon pine needles
- 2 teaspoons oak leaves
- 1 teaspoon rowan leaves

Grind and empower the herbs and then place them in a small pot with the oil. Swirl the oil over low heat until you can smell the mixture in the air. Let the oil cool and then strain into a jar.

Protection Incense

- 1 teaspoon clover
- 1 tablespoon juniper (leaves and crushed berries)
- 1 teaspoon mistletoe
- 1 teaspoon mint
- 1 tablespoon pennyroyal

Grind herbs, empower them with your intent, and place in a jar.

Warding Incense

- ½ teaspoon clover
- ½ teaspoon juniper (leaves and crushed berries)
- ½ teaspoon mistletoe leaves
- ½ teaspoon field mint or peppermint
- ½ teaspoon pennyroyal

Grind the herbs, empower them with your intent, and place in a jar.

Protection Oil

- 2 teaspoons juniper
- 1 teaspoon mint
- 1 tablespoon vervain
- ¼ cup vegetable oil

Grind and empower the herbs and then place them in a small pot with the oil. Swirl the oil over low heat until you can smell the mixture in the air. Let the oil cool and then strain into a jar.

Protective (Modern) Witch Bottle Brew

- 2 teaspoons nettle
- 2 teaspoons mullein
- 1 teaspoon mint
- 1 teaspoon raspberry leaves

- Pinch of valerian
- 1 cup spring or rain water

Brew this in a cauldron or an iron pot. Follow the basic brewing instructions. This brew can be sprinkled around or worn on the body to offer personal protection.

Psychic Incense

- 1 tablespoon mugwort
- 2 teaspoons eyebright
- 1 tablespoon yarrow
- 1 teaspoon thyme

Grind herbs, empower them with your intent, and place in a jar.

Psychic Oil

- 1 teaspoon eyebright
- 2 teaspoons yarrow
- 1 tablespoon mugwort
- ¼ cup vegetable oil

Grind and empower the herbs and then place them in a small pot with the oil. Swirl the oil over low heat until you can smell the mixture in the air. Let the oil cool and then strain into a jar.

Purification Incense

- 1 tablespoon pine needles
- 1 tablespoon vervain
- 1 tablespoon betony

Grind together the herbs and add a pinch of salt. Empower the mixture with your intent and place in a jar.

Purification Oil

- 1 tablespoon elder flowers
- 1 tablespoon oak leaves
- Pinch of valerian

Grind and empower the herbs and then place them in a small pot with the oil. Swirl the oil over low heat until you can smell the mixture in the air. Let the oil cool and then strain into a jar.

Spirituality Incense

- 1 tablespoon elder leaves
- 1 tablespoon hazel leaves
- 1 tablespoon mugwort
- 1 drop of spirituality oil

Grind the herbs together and add the drop of oil. Empower the mixture with your desire and spread out to dry. Bottle the incense when it has dried.

Spirituality Oil

- 1 tablespoon elder flowers
- 1 teaspoon crushed hazel nuts
- 2 teaspoons mugwort

Grind and empower the herbs and then place them in a small pot with the oil. Swirl the oil over low heat until you can smell the mixture in the air. Let the oil cool and then strain into a jar.

Unhexing Incense

- 1 tablespoon pine needles
- 1 teaspoon rose
- 2 teaspoons juniper
- 1 tablespoon nettle

Grind herbs, empower them with your intent, and place in a jar.

Unhexing Oil

- 1 teaspoon rose
- 1 tablespoon nettle
- 1 teaspoon vervain
- 1 teaspoon apple blossom
- ¼ cup vegetable oil

Grind and empower the herbs and place them in the pot with oil. Swirl the oil over low heat until you can smell the mixture in the air. Let the oil cool and then strain into a jar.

Sleeping Potion

- 1 tablespoon valerian
- 1 tablespoon hops
- 1 tablespoon chamomile
- 2 teaspoons mugwort
- 1½ cups water

Mix and empower the herbs and brew. Drink an eight-ounce cupful before going to bed. This potion is quite effective, but tastes bitter; I recommend adding sugar.

Nerve Tonic

- 1 teaspoon yarrow
- 1 teaspoon marjoram
- 1 teaspoon nettle
- 1 teaspoon sage
- 2 teaspoons chamomile
  (or 1 chamomile tea bag)
- 1 teaspoon Saint John's wort
- 1 teaspoon thyme
- Pinch hops
- Pinch valerian
- 1½ cups water

Mix and empower the herbs. Brew together and slowly sip an eight-ounce cup of the tonic to relax and calm your nerves after stressful situations.

Stomach Tonic

- 1 teaspoon marjoram
- 1 teaspoon thyme
- 1 teaspoon sage
- 1 tablespoon mullein
- 1 cup water

Mix and empower the herbs and brew. Drink this tonic when feeling nauseous to calm the stomach and flush out the sickness.

Antidiarrhea Tonic
- 2 tablespoons mullein
- 2 tablespoons catnip
- 2 cups water

Grind herbs, empower them with your intent, and place in a jar. Drink two cups in order to bring relief.

Purification Herb Bath
- 1 teaspoon thyme
- 1 teaspoon marjoram
- 1 teaspoon woodruff
- 1 teaspoon parsley
- 1 teaspoon chamomile
- 1 teaspoon mint
- Pinch valerian

Mix herbs, empower them with your intent, and bundle the herbs together in a thin cloth pouch. Place the bundle in your bath water to infuse it with purifying properties.

Cold and Flu Tonic
- 1 tablespoon yarrow
- 1 tablespoon elder flowers
- 1 tablespoon mint
- 1 tablespoon nettle
- 2 cups water

Mix and empower the herbs and brew. Drink one cup every six hours to speed recovery.

Wart Remover Poultice

- Fresh crushed mullein
- Fresh crushed dandelion leaves
- 1 whole dandelion leaf

Mix the crushed mullein and dandelion leaves together and apply it directly to the wart. Cover this with the whole dandelion leaf and cover with a cloth bandage. Replace with a new poultice every day until the wart is gone.

Vision Salve

- 1 tablespoon mugwort
- 1 tablespoon angelica
- ½ teaspoon chicory
- ½ cup shortening

Grind, mix, and empower the herbs; heat them in the shortening. When the mixture has cooled slightly, strain and bottle the ointment for use. Apply a dab of the ointment to the "third eye" area of the forehead and on the wrists before engaging in clairvoyance exercises to boost your abilities.

Banishing Blend

- ½ teaspoon angelica
- ½ teaspoon fumitory
- ½ teaspoon juniper
- ½ teaspoon nettle
- ½ teaspoon Saint John's wort
- ½ teaspoon yarrow
- ½ teaspoon betony

Mix herbs together, empower them, and burn them as incense during banishing rituals.

Zodiac Blends

These herb blends are simple mixtures that are aligned with the elements and qualities of each of the individual signs of the zodiac. They can be either ground together for incense, carried in a cloth pouch for an herbal charm, or added to a half cup of vegetable oil to create a magical oil. In any of the options, use equal parts of the herbs—one tablespoon of each to create the proper blends.

Aries: juniper, nettle, peppermint

Taurus: rose, thyme, yarrow

Gemini: marjoram, mint, parsley

Cancer: moonwort, rose, willow leaves

Leo: juniper, mistletoe, oak leaves

Virgo: caraway, peppermint, thyme

Libra: apple blossom, marjoram, mint

Scorpio: blackthorn, heather, nettle

Sagittarius: cinquefoil, juniper, maple

Capricorn: comfrey, oak moss, vervain

Aquarius: mint, sage, valerian

Pisces: catnip, rose hips, seaweed

Conclusion

I've now shown the hows, whats, and whys of the magic, but there are two more things to cover. The first is repetition; occasions will occur when you will have to cast a spell several times, such as every night for a week leading up to the full moon, in order for your desire to manifest. Needing to repeat a spell doesn't mean that you did it wrong the first time or that you don't have enough power. There can be many reasons why you would need to repeat a spell. Sometimes when you are working for a large-scale intention, many probabilities and situations need to be altered in order for your goal to reach fruition. Spells work by using radiant life energy charged with intent, so the more energy you send out, the larger a goal you can work toward. This level of magic is difficult even for a group of people, especially if the spell is only cast once. Repetition creates a stronger current of energy that continually feeds your goal over a long period of time, which can be ideal in cases of healing work or binding spells.

The other thing to remember is the need for mundane effort. You can cast a powerful spell to gain employment, but if you never take the steps to find a new job, it is highly unlikely that you will have one fall in your lap. Magic helps change us and the world around us. If we don't make a mundane effort to connect to the world around us, we won't be involved in the change; even though our magic can create opportunity, we can't claim it if we're not tapped into it. That being said, let me assure you that with a bit of training, magic, and effort, your goals can be realized in amazing ways. Mundane effort is not necessary or even possible in the fulfillment of certain spells. I've used magic to get someone to communicate with me, to ease pain, etc. In those types of cases, mundane efforts were not possible or needed. Magic works all by itself, but effort speeds your success.

I hope that you have found the training and magic in this book both useful and enjoyable. Living a magical life is a wonderful journey and all of your efforts in training will be rewarding. Magical ability and spiritual understanding are your birthright, but with power comes responsibility and consequence. Your actions affect those around you. Treat all creatures with respect and try to live in balance. Strive for harmony and remember that inner peace is derived from the love and security found within—not from outside influences or peer approval—and that inner peace, love, and security are the most important things in life. May the power of magic bring you all that's right for you, in goodness and for the good of all. Blessed be.

Appendices

appendix one

Index of Spells and Rituals

Charms

Crystal and Gem Magic

Witch Bottles

Magical Safekeeping

Nature Magic

appendix two

Tables of Correspondences

Planet	Sign	Day	Element	#	Herbs	Stones	Metals	Color	Intents
Sun	Leo	Sun.	Fire	1	Angelica, Ash, Chamomile, Chicory, Eyebright, Hazel, Juniper, Mistletoe, Oak, Rowan, St. John's Wort, Walnut	Citrine, Diamond, Topaz, Tiger Eye	Gold	Yellow	Power, Authority, Protection

Mercury	Gemini/ Virgo	Wed.	Air/ Earth	3	Aspen, Caraway, Clover, Elecampane, Fern, Marjoram, Mint, Parsley	Agate, Amber	Aluminum /Mercury	Orange	Communication, Health, Learning, Speech
Venus	Taurus/ Libra	Fri.	Earth/ Air	2	Alder, Apple, Barley, Birch, Blackberry, Catnip, Coltsfoot, Cowslip, Elder, Feverfew, Foxglove, Heather	Emerald, Rose Quartz, Jade	Copper	Pink, Green, Copper	Love, Beauty, Attraction
Moon	Cancer	Mon.	Water	9	Kelp, Club moss, Grape, Irish moss, Loosestrife, Moonwort, Potato, Turnip, Willow	Moon-stone, Selenite	Silver	Silver	Psychic power, Feminine energy, Gentle healing
Mars	Aries	Tues.	Fire	5	Broom, Gorse, Hawthorn, Holly, Hops, Pennyroyal, Peppermint, Pine, Sloe, Woodruff	Ruby, Carnelian	Iron	Red	Force, War, Masculine energy, Power, Protection

Jupiter	Sagittarius	Thur.	Fire	8	Avens, Betony, Cinquefoil, Dandelion, Linden, Maple, Meadow-sweet, Sage	Sapphire, Lapis, Amethyst	Tin	Blue	Luck, Money, Influence, Legal matters, Success
Saturn	Capricorn	Sat.	Earth	4	Belladonna, Comfrey, Fumitory, Hellebore, Hemp, Ivy, Mullein, Poplar, Yew	Onyx, Obsidian, Garnet	Lead	Indigo, Brown	Binding, Time, Age, Teaching, Protection
Uranus	Aquarius	Wed.	Air	7		Turquoise, Clear quartz	White Gold, Lime, Uranium	White	Genius, Madness, Technology, Electricity
Neptune	Pisces	Fri.	Water	6		Opal, Coral, Aquama-rine, Beryl	Platinum	Opal-escent	Dreams, Psychic work, Visions, Drugs
Pluto	Scorpio	Tues.	Water	0		Jet, Black coral, Coal	Chrome	Black	Breaking Limits, Binding, Protection

bibliography

Buckland, Raymond. *Practical Candleburning Rituals: Spells and Rituals for Every Purpose.* St. Paul: Llewellyn Publications, 1982.

———. *Advanced Candle Magick: More Spells and Ritual for Every Purpose.* St. Paul: Llewellyn Publications, 2002.

———. *Signs, Symbols and Omens: An Illustrated Guide to Magical and Spiritual Symbolism.* St. Paul: Llewellyn Publications, 2003.

Cabot, Laurie. *Power of the Witch: The Earth, The Moon, and The Magical Path to Enlightenment.* New York: Delta, 1989.

Conway, D.J. *A Little Book of Candle Magic*. New York: Crossing Press, 2000.

Cunningham, Scott. *Magical Herbalism: The Secret Craft of the Wise*. St Paul: Llewellyn Publications, 2002.

———. *Cunningham's Encyclopedia of Magical Herbs*. St. Paul: Llewellyn Publications, 2003.

———. *The Complete Book of Incense, Oils, and Brews*. St. Paul: Llewellyn Publications, 2003.

De Angeles, Ly. *Witchcraft: Theory and Practice*. St. Paul: Llewellyn Publications, 2000.

Dunwich, Gerina. *The Wicca Spellbook: A Witch's Collection of Wiccan Spells, Potions, and Recipes*. New York: Citadel Press, 1994.

Furie, Blackthorn. *The Black Book: A Witch's Guide to Tradition*. Baltimore: Publish America, 2010.

Grimassi, Raven. *The Witches' Craft*. St. Paul: Llewellyn Publications, 2002.

K, Amber. *True Magic: A Beginner's Guide*. St. Paul: Llewellyn Publications, 1990.

Malbrough, Ray T. *Charms, Spells, and Formulas*. St. Paul: Llewellyn Publications, 1986.

Morgan, Annalynn M., ed. *Quantum Entanglements*. Hauppauge: Nova Publishers, 2012.

Penczak, Christopher. *Instant Magic: Ancient Wisdom, Modern Spellcraft*. St. Paul: Llewellyn Publications, 2006.

Sheba, Lady. *The Grimoire of Lady Sheba.* St Paul: Llewellyn
   Publications, 2001.

Skelton, Robin. *The Practice of Witchcraft Today.* New York:
   Citadel Press, 1990.